FROM BROKENNESS TO ATONEMENT, FAITH, HOPE AND LOVE

A Vietnam War Sniper's Journey and a

Psychiatrist's Bibliotherapy

HANI RAOUL KHOUZAM, MD, MPH, FAPA

Publisher's Name: Hani Raoul Khouzam, MD, MPH, FAPA

ISBN: 978-1-968442-29-3

TABLE of CONTENTS

To all the veterans who sacrificed their life to protect the nation.

In gratitude to my late father, Raoul; my late mother, Jeannette; and thankfulness to my sisters, Hoda and Héla; my brother, Hadi; my wife, Lynn; and my children, Andrew, Adam, Andrea; and son-in-law, Nic; and granddaughters, Abigail and Liliana.

In memory and acknowledgment of my teachers, mentors, instructors, and supervisors.

A word fitly spoken is like apples of gold in settings of silver.

—Proverbs 25:1

C H A P T E R 1

MR. L'S UNTIMELY LEFT-EYE SURGERY

Mr. L was a single male veteran who never married and who had no children. He served with the United States Army during the Vietnam War. When he was forty-four years old, he presented to the emergency room of the Veteran Hospital in Manchester, New Hampshire, with a recent left-eye injury that he sustained in a motorcycle accident. The seriousness of the injury led to his immediate hospitalization and the performance of a left-eye retinal detachment surgery, which was successful and uneventful.

During his surgical recovery period, he fell asleep. An urgent psychiatric consultation was requested with a very specific request of prescribing a medication that could be administrated to prevent his rapid eye movements (REMs), which occurred when he was deeply asleep. The consultation request emphasized that any delay in preventing REM would jeopardize the recent retinal repair and could result in left-eye blindness.

On that day, I was the psychiatrist on call duty and was surprised to experience reactions of irritability and frustration toward this psychiatric consultation because REM is a normal stage of sleep that is most associated with dreaming in which the brain and body act very different than they do during other stages of sleep. During REM, the skeletal muscles act as if they are paralyzed. In fact, all voluntary muscles, except for eye muscles, are atonic or without movement. This is an important benefit as

1

it protects the sleeping person and others from injury; otherwise, people would act out their dreams.

Because it is inherently obvious that waking up a sleeping person would instantly halt their REM, and to my knowledge, there has never been any established correlation between REM sleep and delayed healing following a retinal detachment surgery. The known factors that have been associated with a good, final visual prognosis include timely treatment, prompt surgery, shorter length of laceration, and better-presenting visual acuity.[1] A review of medical records confirmed that Mr. L did meet all these criteria and there was no risk associated with his REM sleep, causing any complication or delay in healing his left eye retina.

An Unseasonable Request

A prompt response to this psychiatric consultation would result in my missing a special documentary on the life and death of former Egypt's president Anwar al-Sadat, who was assassinated on the sixth of October 1981, during a special military parade in Cairo, Egypt (see figure 1). The military parade was a memorial event that is annually celebrated to commemorate Egypt's military forces advance to liberate the Sinai Peninsula (see figure 2) from Israel's occupation and occurred on the sixth of October 1973, and it coincided on that year with the observance of Yom Kippur, the Jewish remembrance of the day of atonement.[2] This untimely request for an unseasonable psychiatric consultation led me to reflect on Yom Kippur and the long complicated history of the Arabs and Israelis' conflict.

---

1   Gokce G., Sobaci G., Ozgonul C., *Post-traumatic Endophthalmitis: A Mini Review. Seminars in Ophthalmology* (2015), 30(5-6): 470–474.

2   Rabinovich, *The Yom Kippur War* (Schocken Books, 2004), 498.

Fig. 1. Egypt's President Anwar al-Sadat standing prior to his assassination

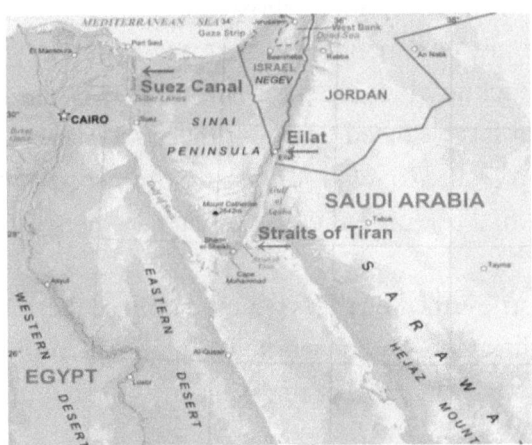

Fig. 2. The Sinai Peninsula location between Egypt and Israel

Yom Kippur and the Meaning of Atonement

Yom Kippur, or the Day of Atonement, is the annual Jewish observance of fasting, prayer, and repentance. It is considered the holiest day on the Jewish calendar. In three separate passages in the Holy Scripture, the Jewish people are told, "The tenth day of the seventh month is the Day of Atonement. It shall be a sacred occasion for you. You shall practice self-denial."[3]

During that day, fasting is seen as a fulfilling of a biblical commandment since it enables the believers to put aside their physical desires in order to concentrate on their spiritual needs through prayer, repentance, and self-improvement. Yom Kippur is a moment in time when the mind, body, and soul are dedicated to the reconciliation with God, other fellow human beings, and oneself. The believers are commanded to turn to those whom they have wronged first, acknowledging their sins toward others and the pain that they might have caused them. At the same time, they must be willing to forgive and to let go of certain offenses and the feelings of resentment that are provoked by others.

On this journey, the believers become both seekers and givers of pardon. Only then God would be asked to grant his forgiveness. "And for all these, God of forgiveness, forgive, pardon, and grant atonement.

"[4]In a tactical and strategic move, President Sadat's unexpected attack on Yom Kippur took the Israeli Army by surprise. It was the first time, since the founding of Israel as a nation in 1948, that an Arab leader dared to attack the well-equipped and outstandingly

---

3   *New International Version*, "Leviticus 23:27" (Grand Rapids, Michigan: Zondervan, 2012)

4   *New International Version*, "Genesis 15:18" (Grand Rapids, Michigan: Zondervan, 2012).

trained Israeli military forces.

The Arabs and Israelis' Conflict

The origins of Arabs and Israelis' conflict date back to the scriptures when Jehovah God promised to Abraham's "seed" the land "from the river of Egypt to the great river of Euphrates." This promise is considered valid for Arabs and Jews alike through their lineage from Abraham's sons, Ishmael, the father of the Arabs, and Isaac, the father of the Jews. Prior to 1000 BC and since the reign of the early Hebrew kings, this promised Holy Land has been a battleground for a succession of conquests by Assyrians, Babylonians, Persians, Greeks, Ptolemies, Syrians, Romans, Muslims, Crusaders, Seljuk Turks, Mameluke Egyptians, Ottoman Turks, and even the British, who ruled that land for twenty-five years, following World War I, and by that time was called Palestine. Through it all, the Arabs and the Jews have survived in relative peace and they have maintained a cultural and religious attachment to their ancestral home, which was inhabited by the Arabs for two thousand years.

Beginning in the 1860s, there were groups of European Jews who promoted migration to the Holy Land. In 1897, a Central European journalist, Theodor Herzl, challenged the First World Zionist Congress to develop a program for creating a Jewish homeland in Palestine. In 1916, the British and the French secretly negotiated the Sykes-Picot Agreement, which provided supervisory roles over various areas of the Arab world and wherein the British were given responsibility for Palestine. In 1917, in a one-page letter from Britain's Lord Balfour, which is historically known as the Balfour Declaration to Lord Rothschild, he bolstered the Zionist concept and expressed British sentiments: "His Majesty's government view with favor the establishment in Palestine of a home for the Jewish people." A gesture for the Arabs was included to the effect

5

that "nothing shall be done which may prejudice the civil and religious rights of existing non-Jewish communities in Palestine."

The Arabs, who outnumbered the Jews ten-to-one at that time, considered the proposed arrangement extremely unfair. The debates concerning the possibility of a Jewish state became even more bitter. In 1923, British administrators and occupation forces were installed in Palestine and became immediately aware of an emerging conflict between groups of immigrant Jews, who were claiming the Holy Land as theirs, and the long-settled Arab majority, who resented the intrusion. Hitler's drive to exterminate the German Jews in the 1930s and the 1940s gave further impetus to Palestine's growth, and Zionism became a worldwide force, encouraging Jews to migrate to the Holy Land.

The Arabs saw themselves as being forced to give up much of their lands to Jewish settlers as part of an international effort to compensate the Jews for the suffering they had endured prior and during the genocide. The situation grew even more intense at the end of World War II, when Arabs and Jews in their drives for nationalism were in direct opposition to one another. Their struggles surfaced at about the same time in the territory of Palestine. Peaceful coexistence began to erode on the political level when the Arabs sensed that the growing Jewish settlements would eventually unite in some kind of political entity and the Arabs would become a minority in their own homeland.

With the end of World War II, the United Nations moved officially to create a Jewish State, and in 1947, the partition of Palestine was initiated, which gave 54 percent of the land area to the Jews, who represented but one third of the population and owned only 10 percent of the land. Neither the Palestinian Arabs nor the neighboring Arab states found the plan acceptable. the Jews, however, accepted the partition. The struggle between the Arabs and the Jews intensified, especially when the British mandate ended in 1948 and hundreds of thousands of Jews moved into Palestine without the Arabs consent.

Israel's Birth as a Nation

On May 14, 1948, the Jews proclaimed the birth of their new country, the State of Israel. With British forces gone, the civil war that had been smoldering between the Jews and Arabs in Palestine erupted in a violent conflict. Nearly half a million Palestinian Arabs fled the war zone into adjacent Arab countries, expecting to return to their homes following an Arab victory. That victory did not materialize, and the vast majority of those Arab refugees were forced out of the newly created state of Israel.

The United Nations brought about an armistice in 1949, but this did not bring real peace. A propaganda war developed and sporadic border incidents and terrorism continued. The Palestinian Arabs did not form a state, and neither the Israelis nor the United Nations could bring them to the peace table. Meanwhile, the Israelis asserted their military superiority and drove the Arabs into deeper bitterness and frustration.

The 1956 Suez Canal Crisis

A new crisis arose in 1956 when the president of Egypt, Gamal Abdel Nasser, nationalized the Suez Canal. Israel saw this action as an opportunity to retaliate for border raids and to force the Arabs to recognize Israel as a state. With British support, Israeli forces invaded the Sinai and, under French air cover, rolled their tanks swiftly across the Sinai Peninsula to the Suez Canal and into the southern tip of the Sinai at Sharm el-Sheikh. Under pressure from the United Nations, the British and French pulled out and the Israelis retreated from the Sinai with the assurance that the United States would prevent Egypt from interfering with Israeli shipping through the Straits of Tiran (see figure 2). Historically and traditionally, most of the Arab states often disagreed with each other on many matters, their only one point of unity was to defeat Israel, even though they could not agree on the best means of accomplishing this unifying goal.

The Six-Day War

An era of relative calm prevailed between Israel and its Arab neighbors during the late 1950s and early 1960s; however, the political climate remained unsettled. Arab leaders were still disappointed and bitter by their military losses and the hundreds of thousands of Palestinian refugees created by Israel's 1948 war. Many Israelis, meanwhile, continued to believe that they were facing an existential threat from their neighbors, especially Egypt and other Arab nations.

By the mid-1960s, Syrian backed Palestinian guerillas were staging attacks across the Israeli border, provoking reprisal raids from the Israel Defense Forces. In April 1967, the skirmishes worsened after Israel and Syria fought a ferocious air and artillery engagement in which six Syrian fighter jets were destroyed. In the wake of this battle, the Soviet Union provided Egypt with intelligence, suggesting that Israel was moving troops to its northern border with Syria in preparation for a full-scale invasion. Although the information was not confirmed, it nevertheless stirred Egyptian president Gamal Abdel Nasser (see figure 3), who announced that an attack on any Arab state would be considered an attack on Egypt, and he began a massive troop buildup on the Sinai- Israeli border, hoping to deter the Israelis from attacking Syria. Nasser also requested the removal of the United Nations peacekeeping

Fig. 3. President Gamal Abdel Nasser in a patriotic speech announcing his support for Syria

forces that had been guarding the border with Israel for over a decade. He mobilized the Egyptian troops into the area and took control of Sharm el-Sheikh at the Straits of Tiran (see figure 2). On May 22, Egypt banned Israeli shipping from the Straits of Tiran, and a week later, Nasser sealed a defense pact with King Hussein of Jordan (see figure 4).

Fig. 4. King Hussein of Jordan announcing his pact with President Nasser of Egypt

As the situation in the Middle East deteriorated, American president Lyndon B. Johnson cautioned both sides against firing the first shot and attempted to garner support for an international maritime operation to reopen the Straits of Tiran. The plan never materialized, and the Israeli cabinet concluded that the only course against Nasser's actions was to launch a war. On June 5, 1967, Israeli forces, under its minister of defense, Moshe Dayan, made a predawn, preemptive attack by initiating Operation Focus, a coordinated aerial attack on Egypt. That morning, some 200 Israeli fighter jets swooped west over the Mediterranean before converging on Egypt from the north. After catching the Egyptians by surprise, they assaulted eighteen different airfields and eliminated roughly 90 percent of the Egyptian Air Force as it sat on the ground. Israel then expanded the range of its attack and decimated the air forces of Jordan, Syria, and Iraq.

The relative success of Operation Focus caused Israel to exaggerate the importance of air power at the expense of artillery. Operation Focus also caused a fixation on the idea of destroying air bases—the destruction of most of Egypt's air forces and air defenses, thus allowing a ground war invasion of Egypt and gaining control over the Sinai Peninsula and Gaza Strip from Egypt. A simultaneous attack invaded Syria and took part of its territory—the Golan Heights. At the same time, Israel attacked Jordan and captured the West Bank and East Jerusalem where the Palestinians were predominantly living since the creation of the Israeli state in 1948.

In six days, which was later described in many commentaries as the six days war, Israel roughly tripled the size of its territory (see figure 5) and established settlements in Gaza, the Sinai Peninsula, and the West Bank, which right wing Israelis refer to by the biblical names Judea and Samaria and consider these occupied territories to be the biblical lands of the Jewish people. The Arabs insisted that they were only preparing for a possible Israeli strike, and that this war, like the others, was just another step in the Israeli plans for conquest of the Arab people. The Egyptian president Gamal Abdel Nasser said, "War between us and Israel is inevitable," but evidently, he could not predict that, in its early stages, the six days war would cost the Arabs 15,000 soldiers, two billion dollars' worth of material, and 26,000 square miles of Arab land and unfortunately did not bring any peace but rather cemented more resentment toward Israel and its Western world, European and American allies.

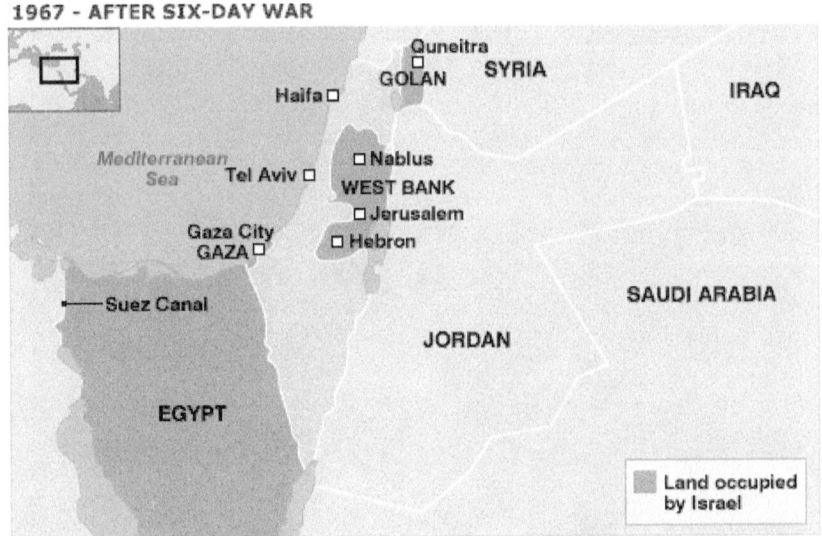

Fig. 5. Israel occupation of territories after the six-day war

President Anwar al-Sadat and the Changing Dynamics of the Arabs and Israelis' Conflict

The sixth of October War of 1973 began when a coalition of Egyptian and Syrian forces launched a joint surprise attack on Israel on Yom Kippur, the holiest day in Judaism, which coincided that year with the observance of the Muslim holy month of Ramadan. Egyptian and Syrian forces crossed cease-fire lines respectively and Egypt's armed forces advanced to the Israeli-held Sinai Peninsula (see figure 6), which was captured from Egypt, following its six-day war in June of 1967. By the time of the Yom Kippur War, the Arab states had learned the lessons of Operation Focus. Air defense was provided by antiaircraft missiles, and planes were kept in protected hangars. Attacks on air fields became largely irrelevant.

Fig. 6. Egyptian Armed Forces advancing to the Sinai
Peninsula for its liberation

For Sadat and the Egyptians, the sixth of October War of 1973 was
a victory, as the initial Egyptian successes restored Egyptian pride
and led to peace talks with the Israelis that eventually led to Egypt
regaining the entire Sinai Peninsula in exchange for Egypt-Israel
peace treaty. This then led to Egypt estrangement from most other
Arab countries who denounced Sadat as a traitor of the Palestinian
cause and eventually led to the plot of his assassination on the sixth
of October 1981.[5]

While waiting with anxious anticipation to watch the documentary
about the plot of his assassination and the issuing international
events, I was called to see Mr. L for a psychiatric consultation.
Overwhelmed with disappointment and frustration, I forgot
to consider recording the documentary, which was about to be
broadcasted on the local national public television station.

---

5   PJ Vatikiotis, *The History of Modern Egypt*, 4th edition (Baltimore: Johns Hopkins
University 1992), 443.

Chariots of Fire

Although I missed watching the documentary about the life and death of President Sadat, unbeknown to me, my wife, Lynn, had a surprise waiting for me. She had recorded *Chariots of Fire*, one of my favorites and most inspiring movies, which was nominated for seven Academy Awards and ended up winning four, including the award for Best Picture. The film is an epic saga of two athletic runners, Harold Abrahams and Eric Liddell, who, after many years of training and racing, were accepted to represent Great Britain in the 1924 Olympics in Paris. Abrahams, the son of a wealthy Jewish financier, arrives at the University of Cambridge and becomes the first sprinter to complete the trinity Great Court Run—to circle the courtyard in the time it takes for the clock to strike twelve, beginning at the first chime. In addition to winning national running contests, Abrahams becomes involved with a Gilbert and Sullivan company and fell in love with the soprano singer Sybil Gordon.

In the meantime, in Scotland, Eric Liddell, the son of Scottish missionaries, also engages in running competitions. though his sister Jennie fears that running will distract him from pursuing his missionary work, Liddell felt that by his running and his victories, he glorifies God, who created him as a fast runner. Eventually, Abrahams and Liddell meet in a British open race, and Liddell wins. The driven Abrahams is crushed at his defeat, but the renowned professional trainer Sam Mussabini offers to teach and train him to run faster than Liddell. The Cambridge college masters, Sir John Gielgud and Lindsay Anderson, think accepting professional coaching is ungentlemanly, but Abrahams sees their objections as anti-Semitic and hypocritical since they pride themselves on Cambridge's superiority in academic and athletic achievements. Liddell, Abrahams, and the Cambridge runners

Lord Andrew Lindsay, Aubrey Montague, and Henry Stallard are chosen for the British Olympic team.

As they depart for Paris, Liddell learns that he hundred-meter heat in which he was to compete is to be held on Sunday. Because of his deeply held religious convictions, he announces that he will not compete on Sunday, the day of the Sabbath, and he resists the arguments made by the Prince of Wales and the British Olympic Committee. To resolve this impasse, Lord Andrew Lindsay, who already won an Olympic medal in an earlier race, offers to yield his place in the four hundred-meter race scheduled for the following Thursday to Liddell, and he accepted.

At the games, American runner Charles Paddock easily outpaces Abrahams to win the two hundred-meter race, but Abrahams is triumphant in the hundred-meter contest, winning the gold medal. Liddell is not expected to do well at the four hundred- meter distance, but he, nonetheless, wins the gold medal. Following the return of the Olympic team from France to England, Abrahams reunites with his girlfriend, Sybil Gordon, and Liddell pursues his missionary work in China.

Later, Abrahams became the elder statesman of British athletics while Liddell was mourned by all of Scotland following his death in Japanese-occupied China. The striking contrast between Harold Abrahams's motivation and strife to win at any cost versus Eric Liddell's dedication to running as a means to glorify God has guided several of my clinical interventions when addressing patient struggles in achieving success, fulfilling their life purpose, and being accepted for pursuing their aspirations rather than being molded into what society expects them to be.

President Sadat and His Atonement

The sixth of October War of 1973 coincided with the Muslim observance of the month of Ramadan, which is the ninth month of the Islamic lunar calendar. It begins with the sighting of the new moon, after which all physically mature and healthy Muslims are instructed to fast for the complete month. Fasting is done as an act of worship and obedience to Allah (God). During the month of Ramadan from dawn until dusk, Muslims abstain from all food, drinks, and indulging in any that is in excess or pleasurable activities. In addition to its physical component, the spiritual aspects of the fast include an added emphasis on refraining from gossip, lies, obscenity, and, in general, any sinful act. So, during the month of Ramadan, fasting becomes a shield from sins and the fire of hell. A fasting person avoid arguments, fights, and hurts.

President Sadat considered himself a devout and practicing Muslim, could have felt guilty for attacking Israel during the month of Ramadan? Did he endure that guilt and did not experience any relief from its spiritual burden, even when he was jointly awarded with Israel's prime minister Menachem Begin the Nobel Peace Prize in 1978!

Despite credible security warnings, Sadat refused to wear bulletproof vests and confidently argued, "I am among my sons." Seconds before his assassins' bullets ripped through his body, when the attackers approached him with their firing riffles,"he stood saluting them, thinking that they were part of the military parade." (see figure 1)

Was that President Sadat's atonement for attacking his enemies on Yom Kippur during the month of Ramadan? Only eternity could provide the answer to this massacre of a man who was recognized worldwide as a peacemaker with his long former enemy, the nation of Israel.

The October War of 1973 illustrated how war can be an instrument to accomplish peace, which could not be achieved by other means. Other than President Sadat, few would have predicted that a peace treaty between Egypt and Israel could be reached as a result of a fourth Arab-Israeli war.ᶜWhen the Egyptian president addressed the Israeli Knesset on November 20, 1977, he acknowledged his responsibility to employ any instrument necessary to achieve this peace, saying,

God Almighty has made it my fate to assume responsibility on behalf of the Egyptian people… the main duty of which, dictated by responsibility, is to exploit all and every means in a bid to save my Egyptian Arab people and the pan-Arab nation from the horrors of new suffering and destructive wars, the dimensions of which are foreseen only by God Himself.

President Sadat could finally conclude his address in Jerusalem with the Arabic words *Salam Aleikum,* which means "peace be upon you."

---

6   Anwar El Sadat, *In Search of Identity: An Autobiography* (Harper and Row, 1977), 331–332.

C H A P T E R 2

KNOWING FRENCH SAVED THE DAY

Stopping REM Sleep—You Must Be Kidding!

I accepted the current reality and sadly abandoned my wishes to watch President Sadat's special documentary and dragged my feet and went to Mr. L's hospital bed with a foreboded knowledge that the only intervention to stop his REM sleep[7] was to awaken him from his current stage of sleep, which would deprive him from a much-needed rest and could delay or even prevent the healing of his retinal detachment. Mr. L was sound asleep in a post-surgery recovery bed, surrounded by two nurses who appeared anxious. They asked me to urgently order "without any delay" a psychiatric medication that would stop his current episode of REM sleep. They also assertively challenged my understanding of the surgical procedure known as *pneumatic retinopexy* (see figure 7), to which I immediately confirmed my total ignorance.[8]

---

7   Ferini-Strambi L., Zucconi M., *REM Sleep Behavior Disorder,* Clinical *Neurophysiology*(2000), 111 Suppl 2: S136–S134.

8   Petrushkin H. J., Elgohary M. A., Sullivan P. M., *Rescue Pneumatic Retinopexy in Patients with Failed Primary Retinal Detachment Surgery, Retina* (2015), 35(9): 1851–1859.

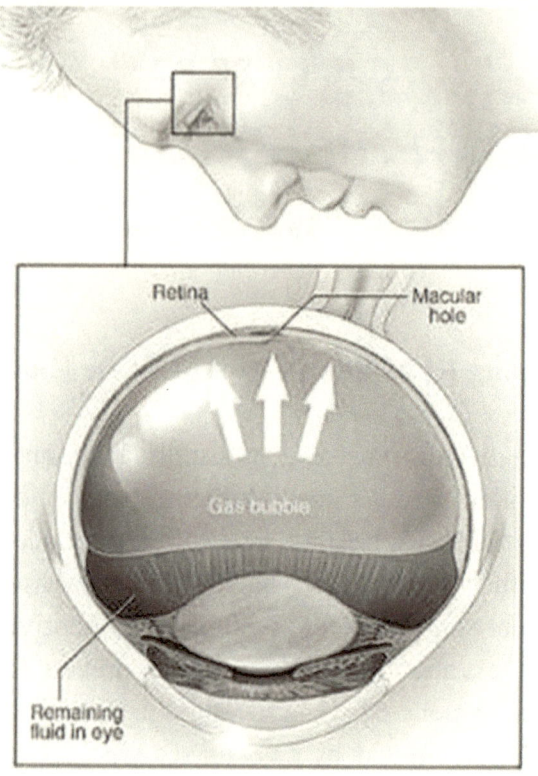

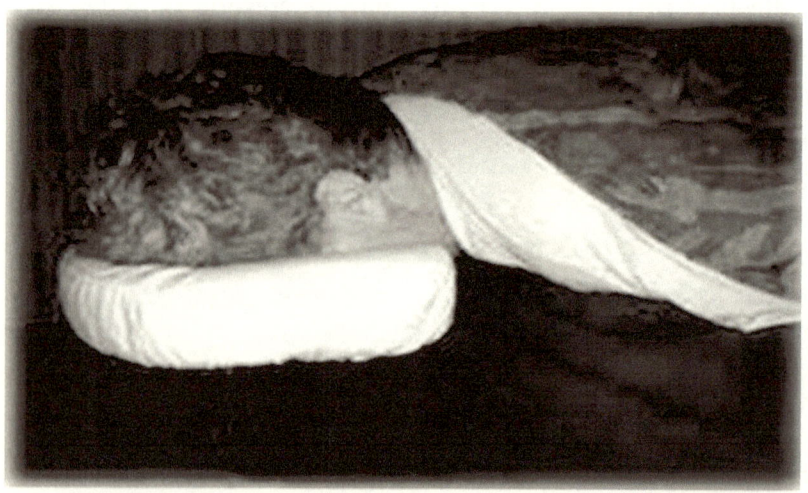

Fig. 7. Pneumatic retinopexy—head down position

Later on, I read about it, and it describes a procedure in which an injected gas bubble seals the detached retinal area to prevents fluid leaking (see figure 7). The nurses' anxiety was instantly manifested in nonverbal expressions of disgust, and they loudly announced, "Any eye movements will adversely affect the gas bubble and delay healing." They added, "You cannot wake him up because he is dreaming in Vietnamese!"

I attempted (to no avail) to assure the nurses that REM sleep will soon end and that it seems that Mr. L was experiencing a pleasant dream because he was singing "Happy Birthday" in French. Furiously, they both left the bedside and brought back their reinforcement— the attending eye surgeon, who happened to be Scottish—and he asked me politely but assertively in French to do something to prevent REM sleep with any of my many arsenals of psychiatric and *magical* medications?

The Cairo-Jesuit School French Education

For the first time in many years, I felt the blessings of knowing the French language, which I learned in my elementary and secondary school education at the *Collège de la Sainte Famille* in Egypt.

The Collège de la Sainte Famille, often abbreviated as *CSF* and referred to as *Jésuites*, is a private Jesuit French school for boys in the Faggala suburb of Cairo in Egypt. It was originally founded in 1879, after a request by Pope Leo XIII for a seminary to help prepare students to become priests in the Catholic Church. The seminary was later moved to a different location, and the building and its surrounding grounds were transformed to a school campus which offers education for boys, mainly in French (see figure 8).

Fig. 8. Collège de la Sainte Famille and its Adjacent Sanctuary Building

Students begin attending classes in that building after six years of primary school and until they complete high school. Along with the primary teaching in the French language, the Arabic language is taught from an early age and then in the secondary stage of education the English language is introduced. All exams are written and prepared in French except for the Arabic language tests and the history and geography courses. The school also offers an optional French curriculum, and when it is successfully completed, the student will earn the prestigious French diploma, *baccalauréat Français*.

During my years of attendance, the school had an average number of 600 students, and some of them were children of foreign diplomats from several countries, which included France, Belgium, Lebanon, Syria, Italy, Greece, England, Spain, Switzerland, Yugoslavia, Armenia, Turkey, Greece, Czechoslovakia, Iran, and Ghana.

Four decades later, my son, Adam, also had reminded me about the Jesuits' core values, which include:

- Magis: Striving for Excellence
- Women and Men for and with Others: Sharing Gifts, Pursuing Justice, and Concern for the Poor
- Cura Personalis: Care for the Individual Person, Respecting Each Person as a Child of God
- Unity of Heart, Mind, and Soul: Developing the Whole Person
- Ad Majorem Dei Gloriam: For the Greater Glory of God
- Forming and Educating Agents of Change: teaching Behaviors that Reflect Critical Thought and Responsible Action on Moral and Ethical Issues

Jesuit education also empathized that the Jesuit values should never be forced on individuals nor ostracize those who do not prefer to follow them. The practice of these values shaped my appreciation for the unique characteristics of every individual person and most probably sparked my interests in pursuing a profession that validates the preciousness of every human life.

My parents' dedication and financial sacrifice offered me the opportunity to be enrolled in that CSF Jesuit French school. So here I am, so many years later, knowing French came in as an expected blessing and allowed me to communicate with the Scottish eye surgeon and to also recognize that Mr. L was singing in French during his dream. I was left to wonder what different outcome would have resulted if I did not know French. In the midst of my bewilderment about my course of action toward this unneeded consult, my mind was immediately transferred back to Egypt, my beloved home country.

Napoleon Influence on Egypt's Education System

Egypt's history is chronicled through more than 7,000 years, and education played an important role in the early days of the development of the Egyptian society. Up to about 2686 BC, culture was developed through written accounts. The formation of religion and societal structures simultaneously evolved and shaped the progression of Egyptian civilization. Unification of Upper and Lower Egypt gave rise to the age of the Pharaohs, which lasted for many centuries until foreign invasion ended Pharaonic rule in 525 BC.

As early as 323 BC, Alexandria, Egypt, housed one of the world's first and most extensive libraries. The Ancient Library of Alexandria was a pivotal place for scholarship until around 30 BC, when the Romans conquered Egypt. The Romans ruled Egypt up to AD 640, until the Arab conquest of Egypt. At this point, society shifted from a Christian to a Muslim culture and adopted the Arabic language. Temples housed formal education and included subjects in the sciences, medicine, and the arts.

In AD 972, an Islamic system of education was formed through Al-Azhar University, which based its teaching methodology on the tenants of the Muslim holy book—the Qur'an. This act laid the groundwork for the religious education track that still exists today.

Between 868 and 1260, several dynasties ruled Egypt, and were followed by Turkish tribes, who took over until 1517. By that time, the Ottoman Empire conquered Egypt, and until 1798, little emphasis was placed on education. Napoleon was next to exert his power, albeit just for the short span between 1798–1801. His French influence impressed Egyptian life and many private schools in Egypt used French as their primary language of education.

Although English is the main language of higher and graduate education in Egypt and my father, Raoul, was a high school English teacher, my mother, Jeannette, chose to maintain the French education streak, and my parents sent all their children—my older sister, Hoda, and my younger sister, Héla, and my younger brother, Hadi—to French private schools. I am gratefully thankful for the many beneficial effects that my French education had on shaping my worldview, which also allowed me to establish a spontaneous connection with Mr. L.

The France-Scotland Connection

The story of Scotland's relationship with France is older even than the countries themselves. Dating back to 1295, the Auld Alliance was built upon Scotland and France's shared interests in controlling England's aggressive expansion plans. Drawn up by John Balliol of Scotland and Philip IV of France, it was first and foremost a military and diplomatic alliance, but for most ordinary Scots, it brought more obvious benefits through jobs as mercenaries in France's armies and, of course, a steady supply of fine French wines.

Henry V's victory at the Battle of Agincourt in 1415 was one of England's greatest military achievements, but for the French, it was a disaster on such a scale that it led to the near collapse of the country. In desperation, the French Dauphin turned to the Scots— England's traditional enemy—for help. As always, anxious for a fight with the Auld Enemy, more than 12,000 Scots boarded ships bound for France. And they didn't have to wait too long, and in 1421, at the Battle of Bauge, they defeated the English army, killing the Duke of Clarence.

The Auld Alliance wasn't simply a military alliance, but also, a commercial alliance, which was founded on the Scots' love of wine— French wine in particular!

Mary, Queen of Scots, was a very French figure. In 1548, at the age of just five, she left Scotland for France. It was there that she was to spend her formative years. A decade later, she married the heir to the French throne—the Dauphin François.

In July 1559, François succeeded his father, Henri II, and the couple became king and queen of France and Scotland. Although Mary returned to Scotland in 1561, following the death of her husband, she continued to possess and manage considerable French estates—the legacy of the dowry settled upon her as a consequence of her brief marriage. In Scotland, and even during her long imprisonment in England, Mary maintained a predominantly French household and a pronounced interest in French affairs. French was to remain her first language. The original alliance that granted dual citizenship in both countries was eventually revoked by the French government in 1903. Even today, with England exiting the European Union, there are ongoing debates in Scotland about leaving its union with England and becoming an independent country and remaining in the European Union.

The attending eye surgeon, despite his fluency in English, chose to address me in French to assert that he understood that Mr. L was singing "Happy Birthday" in French and not dreaming in Vietnamese. The joyous content of the dream seemed to not matter, and the eye surgeon still insisted on asking me in French to prescribe something that would interrupt REM sleep.

Everyday Clinical Duties of Postoperative Nurses

Postoperative nurses provide intensive care to patients as they awaken from anesthesia surgical procedure. Because they typically have significant experience in a medical-surgical environment or in emergency medicine, they are equipped to identify complications and intervene quickly and swiftly. They evaluate patients' condition and determine if interventions would be needed to manage emerging complications. They usually oversee only a few patients at a time, ensuring each patient's ultimate comforts.

Mr. L was recovering well and did not exhibit any postoperative complications.He had normal vital signs and was breathing comfortably,and the two postoperative nurses assigned to his care may have been expecting some events to transpire that would require their skillful intervention, so when he began to sing while dreaming, they assumed that his sleep REM cycle would cause the dire complication of delaying his retinal detachment healing. That assumption is considered a puzzlement.

At that moment, I recalled Lynn, my wife, often mentioned a special term that illustrates our response to certain unexpected situations as described in the book *Tyranny of the Urgent*.[9]In that book, the author, Charles E. Hummel, argues that there is a regular

---

9   Charles E. Hummel, *Tyranny of the Urgent, InterVarsity Christian Fellowship of the USA* (Downers Grove, Illinois: 1967).

tension between things that are urgent and things that are important and, far too often, the urgent wins. The urgent, though less important, is prioritized, and therefore, the *important* is put on the back burner. The nurses' focus on their perception of an *urgent* event may have blurred their ability to patiently wait until Mr. L spontaneously wake up, thus missing their opportunity to inquire about the circumstances that led to his left-eye injury and getting to know him as an individual person and not just a surgery-recovering patient.

C H A P T E R 3

NO-EYE-CONTACT PSYCHIATRIC INTERVIEW

Prelude

Initially flabbergasted and then enraged by the odd rational and the incongruent nature of this psychiatric consultation, I called the psychiatry department chief of services, Dr. Paul E. Emery (see figure 9), who passed away at the age of ninety-one on September 8, 2013.

Fig. 9. Dr. Paul E. Emery

When I sought Dr. Emery's advice, he was in his seventy

and vibrant as a recent graduate of a medical school. At the age of thirteen, Dr. Emery, who was born in Montreal, Canada, decided he would become a psychiatrist. And so he did. For more than fifty years, he was a gifted, dedicated, hardworking, highly skilled, compassionate psychiatrist who relentlessly treated thousands of patients, helping them to realize a better life than they would have had otherwise. Being a good doctor and good psychiatrist was fundamental to his life and core identity. He trained at Syracuse Psychopathic Hospital, Western New England Psychoanalytic Institute, Yale University and was a National Institute of Mental Health (NIMH) fellow at Austin Riggs Center in Stockbridge, Massachusetts.

To answer his patriotic call, he interrupted his training to serve during the Korean War, where he became a captain, a division psychiatrist and chief of the mental hygiene clinic in the US Army and received commendations for his excellent service. Following his military services, he resumed and successfully completed his psychiatric training, and in 1962, Dr. Emery moved to Concord, New Hampshire, and practiced private psychiatry for more than twenty-three years. During this time, he was a consultant for Concord Hospital, St. Paul's School in Concord, and the Division of Public Health Program on Alcoholism and Drug Abuse in New Hampshire. He was also the medical director for the forensic unit of the New Hampshire State Hospital. Following this, he became the first medical director and then executive director for the federal Bureau of Veterans Affairs' newly legislated first center on stress recovery in Brecksville, Ohio.

Dr. Emery then became the chief of psychiatry at the Manchester, New Hampshire, VA Medical Center where I had the great privilege to learn from him, as my supervisor, mentor, and above it all, a personal friend. He revived the importance of integrating some of the tenants of psychoanalysis in the identification and management of veterans who suffer from posttraumatic stress disorder. He also pioneered the vision of implementing specialized treatment care teams to address the unique needs of veterans with posttraumatic stress disorder also referred to as PCT programs. As a member of the first inaugurated PCT at the Manchester VA Medical Center in New Hampshire, I participated in providing integrated and comprehensive treatment for the veterans who enrolled in the PCT and other mental health treatment programs. I recall with sincere fondness several colleagues and consultants of the Manchester VA Medical Center and to just mention some of many others such as Drs. Michael F. Mayo-Smith, Donald R. Bernard, Roger Pitman, Michael Carvalho, Slavomir Kolada, Perla Kissmeyer, Pamela Grich, and Amy Wallace; the interdisciplinary treatment team of experienced and specialized clinicians, including Dr. Mark Gilbertson and licensed social workers, Ms. Nancy Berry, Ms. Anne Melvin, and Ms. Terrie Raposo; the nurse practitioners, Ms. Susan Field, Ms. Nancy Donnelly and Ms. Marelyn Telles; and the addiction therapists, Mr. Jack Campbell and Mr. Kevin Kelly. Dr. Emery reflectively listened to my complaint about this unjustifiable consult that requested to stop REM sleep without awakening the patient. He wisely advised me, if I agreed, to wake the patient up and to listen to his *narrative.*[10] I was grateful and thankful that, by that time, Mr. L had spontaneously woke up. The two nurses warned me about any repositioning of his head from the postoperative position (see figure 7). I noticed that he had the classical edition of Fyodor Dostoevsky's *Crime and Punishment* (see figure 10) by his hospital bedside table.

---

10   Pereles L., Jackson R., Rosenal T., Nixon L., *Listening with a Narrative Ear: Insights from a Study of Fall Stories in Older Adults, Canadian Family Physician* (2017), 63(1): E44-E50.

Fig. 10. Crime and Punishment

Listening to the Narratives

Attempts to understand patients' perspectives by listening with a narrative ear will help clinicians develop rapport and negotiate interventions that are more acceptable and effective for patients than a traditional interview process.

A clinically oriented interview typically involves interrupting the flow of the narrative by interjecting clarifying questions, editing out irrelevant data, and choosing clinical terminology. This process might eliminate aspects of the narrative that reveal patients' beliefs, values, fears, and expectations—all of which can assist clinicians in finding common ground when negotiating possible interventions.[11]

---

11   Ibid.

By allowing myself to listen, rather than being rushed to intervene, I would experience a fuller appreciation of Mr. L's circumstances and let his storytelling be the way to set the narratives for sharing his life's significant events in the context of exploring his journey of hopes, aspirations, and expectations. His narratives could be complex and affected by various influences of the environment, personal interactions, and developmental stages, still would provide valuable insight into his life and the lives of those he holds dear to his heart and, when combined with compassionate listening ears, could set the stage for a dialogue and a personal rather than a clinical encounter.

Dostoevsky's Crime and Punishment

In the nineteenth century, the Western world moved away from the romanticism found in the works of Alexander Sergeyevich Pushkin in Russia, Johann Wolfgang von Goethe in Germany, William Wordsworth in England, Nathaniel Hawthorne and Edgar Allan Poe in America and shifted toward a modern realistic approach to literature.

While the world was still reading popular romantic novels and love poems, Russia was leading a movement into the new realistic approach to literature. Fyodor Dostoevsky was one of the forerunners of this movement, along with Gustave Flaubert in France and Mark Twain in America.

In *Crime and Punishment*, Dostoevsky describes and illustrates amazing psychological insight of the human condition. Even a person of great conscience would suffer from action of transgressions, and as soon as the crime is committed, torments and unrelenting guilt could engulf every night and every day of life.

Could the presence of this book by Mr. L's bedside shed lights on his life's story and his narratives?[12]

Alternating Speaking French and English

Mr. L responded to my silent pause with a monologue in French, mentioning that he deserved the punishment of losing his evil left eye, which killed the innocents, and that today was his forty-fourth birthday, which he wished would have been his last day on this earth. He then began to speak in English, expressing his deeply felt disappointment and his defeated expectations for surviving the motorcycle accident, which only left him with a left-side facial bruise and left-eye laceration. He then proceeded to describe how his life began when he was abandoned at birth and was placed in a New Hampshire orphanage where he spent his earlier years of growing up. He joined a cadre of older bully kids who taught him how to intimidate and belittle the weaker kids, and he learned and practiced surviving the orphanage's stressful environment with a complete disregard and indifference to other children's physical needs, emotional pain, and sufferings.

After a long pause, which I decided not to interrupt, his tone of voice changed to that of a toddler and spoke in a broken sentence, "I have…always and still…feel detached and…unable to connect with anybody."

Emotional Components of a Mother Tongue

As feeling beings, our emotional thinking is our true first language. Yet, it is incomplete. Through our strives to become

---

12   Pereles L., Jackson R., Rosenal T., Nixon L., *Listening with a Narrative Ear: Insights from a Study of Fall Stories in Older Adults, Canadian Family Physician* (2017), 63(1): E44-E50. and Luborsky L., *A Pattern-setting Terapeutic Alliance Study Revisited, Psychotherapy Research* (2000), 10:17–29.

emotionally and socially competent, we aspire to a life of quality living and are dissatisfied with the mere purpose of just surviving. to achieve this, our second language not only needs but also demands its first language to be complete. When we experience stressors that threatened our survival, our mother tongue becomes our language of expression, and when we feel safe, loved, and appreciated, we may alternate our human expression between our mother tongue and our second acquired language.[13]

Because Mr. L expressed his initial thoughts and emotions in his spoken mother's tongue, English language, it may have coincided with his life of surviving a stressful existence in the orphanage's harsh, emotional environment, while his acquired French second language may have been an expression of happier life existence as exemplified by singing "Happy Birthday" in French.

Mr. L helped me grasp the notion that his mother's tongue, English language, mainly expressed sad emotions in contrast to his acquired joyful French language expressions. I then recalled some of the conversations I had with my sister, Héla, who, as an English and French bilingual teacher in Toronto, Canada, taught high school Francophone students English and Anglophone students French and could always discern which language her students preferred to use to express their underlying predominant emotions. My daughter, Andrea, who is a speech-language pathologist also reminded me that affective disorders in children and adolescents could impair the acquisition of a second language in bilingual individuals. The acute exacerbation of a preexisting mental illness may also lead to a loss of the ability to speak the second language for a period and the regression to the mother tongue as a mode of communication. The effect could

---

13   El-Gabalawi F., Khouzam HR., *The Effect of Mental Illness on Language Regression to the Mother Tongue in Bilingual Teenagers, J Neuropsychiatry Clin Neurosci 21* (2009), 21(1): 88–91.

be lasting since the second language seems to have a critical period of optimal acquisition and proficiency. Thus, the second language is more vulnerable to the effects of mental illness than the mother tongue.

Mr. L seemed to experience opposite effects in expressing his distressing life events with their emotional manifestation in English, and when he is recovering from periods of emotional decompensation, he would express his feelings of wellness and joy in his second acquired, French language!

Attachment and Life in an Orphanage

Every child needs love and attention (see figure 11) that are consistent, while coinciding with appropriate and non-abusive methods of discipline. Stimulation through exposure to developmentally appropriate holding, hugging, conversation, reading, listening to music, and playing with toys are also necessary steps to develop emotional attachment with peers and caregivers.

Fig. 11. Attachment and bonding between mother and child

In crowded, underfunded, and understaffed orphanages, children could feel abandoned and have to fend on their own in order to survive physically and emotionally. They are also at risk for the development of reactive attachment disorder and posttraumatic stress disorder.[14] Most orphanages are not suited to match their environment to each orphan's disposition. Consequently, many children raised in orphanages feel less safe if they develop attachment to other children and caregivers and become vulnerable to develop reactive attachment disorder as a defense against the pain of anticipating future separation and detachment.

Mr. L then stopped talking, and consequently, I found my mind wandering to the realms of psychiatry with its various described diagnostic domains.

---

14   American Psychiatric Association, *Diagnostic and Statistical Manual of Mental Disorders, 5th edition* (Arlinton, Virginia: 2013), 265-268 and 271-280.

Hani Raoul Khouzam, MD, MPH, FAPA

C H A P T E R 4
THE PSYCHIATRIC CLASSIFICATION OF TRAUMA AND STRESSORS

The American Psychiatric Association and Its Publications

As the etiology of psychiatric disorders is still not clearly known, psychiatric conditions are mostly defined categorically by their clinical syndrome. There are ongoing and conflicting debates in the psychiatric literature if psychiatric disorders are valid discrete disease entities, such as the majority of medical diseases, or if they are better studied and understood using dimensional models. There are also ongoing concerns about the validity and reliability of the diagnostic categories, the reliance on superficial symptoms, and the use of artificial dividing lines between categories , possible cultural bias, and medicalization of human distress.

Since the publication of the first edition of the *Diagnostic and Statistical Manual of Mental Disorder* or DSM-I in 1952, the American Psychiatric Association (APA) introduced several revised DSM's editions—DSM-II in 1968, DSM-III in 1980, DSM-III-R in 1987, DSM-IV in 1994, DSM-IV-TR in 2000, and with the latest edition DSM-5, which was published in 2013 and its Text Revision (DSM-5-TR) published in 2022. This edition attempts to offer a common language and standard criteria for the classification of mental disorders that are used by clinicians, researchers, psychiatric drug regulation agencies, health insurance companies, pharmaceutical companies, the legal system, and policy makers.

Although DSM-5 has been praised for standardizing psychiatric diagnostic categories and criteria, it has also generated controversy and criticism, especially from the National Institute of Mental Health, which argues that it represents an unscientific and subjective system of classifying mental disorders. The publication of the DSM, with tightly guarded copyrights, now makes APA over $5 million a year, historically totaling over $100 million.

The Fifth Edition of the Diagnostic and Statistical Manual of Mental Disorder (DSM-5)

With the publication of the fifth edition of the Diagnostic and Statistical Manual of Mental Disorders, commonly known as DSM-5 and its subsequent revision DSM-5-TR, the new category of trauma- and stressor-related disorders was introduced.[15]Reactive attachment disorder (see figure 12 and table 1) and posttraumatic stress disorder (see figure 13 and table 2) were both included under this category.

---

15   American Psychiatric Association, *Diagnostic and Statistical Manual of Mental Disorders, 5ᵗʰ edition* (Arlington, Virginia: 2013), 265-268 and 271-280.

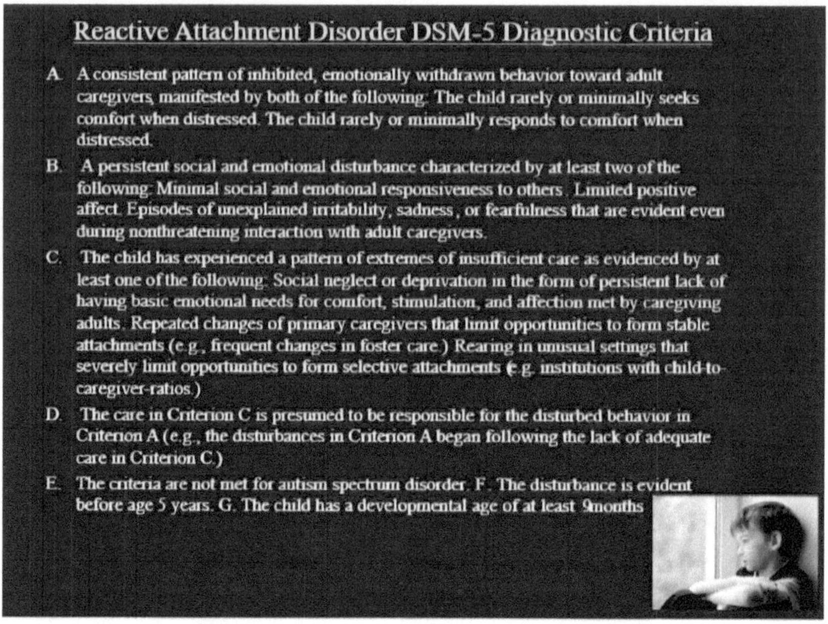

Fig. 12. DSM-5 diagnostic criteria of reactive attachment disorder

Table 1.The DSM-5 diagnostic criteria of reactive attachment disorder (RAD)

Rare or minimal response to comfort when distressed
Minimal social and emotional responses to others
Episodes of unexplained irritability, sadness or tearfulness
Limited expressions of positive affect or joy
Evidence of inadequate basic emotional and social caretaking

A. A consistent pattern of inhibited, emotionally withdrawn behavior toward adult caregivers, manifested by both of the following:

• The child rarely or minimally seeks comfort when distressed.

- The child rarely or minimally responds to comfort when distressed.

B. A persistent social or emotional disturbance characterized by at least two of the following:

- Minimal social and emotional responsiveness to others
- Limited positive affect
- Episodes of unexplained irritability, sadness, or fearfulness that are evident even during nonthreatening interactions with adult caregivers.

C. The child has experienced a pattern of extremes of insufficient care as evidenced by at least one of the following:

- Social neglect or deprivation in the form of persistent lack of having basic emotional needs for comfort, stimulation, and affection met by caring adults
- Repeated changes of primary caregivers that limit opportunities to form stable attachments (e.g., frequent changes in foster care)
- Rearing in unusual settings that severely limit opportunities to form selective attachments (e.g., institutions with high child to caregiver ratios)

D. The care in Criterion C is presumed to be responsible for the disturbed behavior in Criterion A (e.g., the disturbances in Criterion A began following the lack of adequate care in Criterion C).

E. The criteria are not met for autism spectrum disorder.

F. The disturbance is evident before age 5 years

G. The child has a developmental age of at least nine months.

Specify if Persistent:The disorder has been present for more than 12 months.

Specify current severity: Reactive Attachment Disorder is specified as severe when a child exhibits all symptoms of the disorder, with each symptom manifesting at relatively high levels.

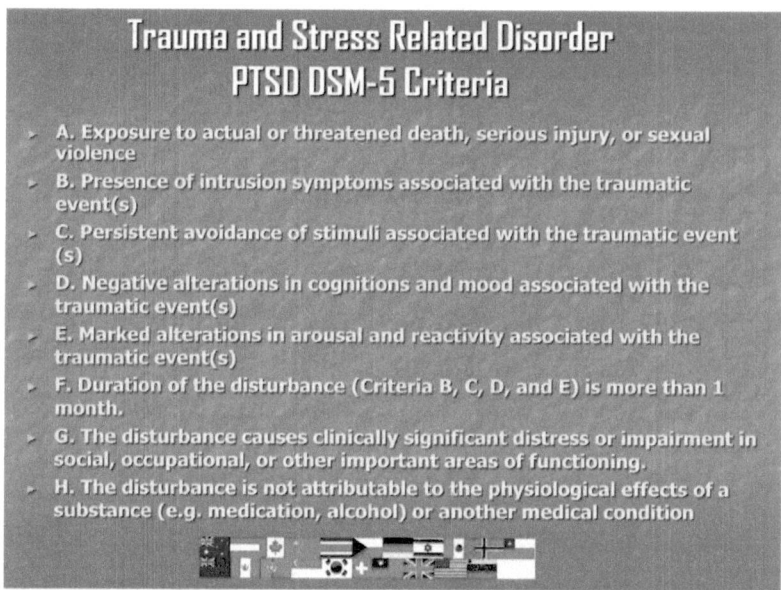

Fig. 13. DSM-5 diagnostic criteria of posttraumatic stress disorder

Table 2. The DSM-5 diagnostic criteria of posttraumatic stress disorder (PTSD)

Exposure to actual or threatened death, serious injury, or sexual violence
Presence of intrusion symptoms associated with the traumatic event(s)

Persistent avoidance of stimuli associated with the traumatic event (s)
Negative alterations in cognitions and mood associated with the traumatic event(s)
Marked alterations in arousal and reactivity associated with the traumatic event(s)
Duration of the disturbance (Criteria B, C, D, and E) is more than 1 month
The disturbance causes clinically significant distress or impairment in social, occupational, or other important areas of functioning
The disturbance is not attributable to the physiological effects of a substance (e.g. medication, alcohol) or another medical condition

Criterion A: Exposure to death, threatened death, serious injury, or sexual violence in one (or more) of the following way(s):

- Direct experience of the trauma
- Witnessing firsthand the trauma
- Learning a relative or close friend was exposed to a trauma
- Repeated or extreme exposure to aversive details of trauma, typically experienced by first responders, medics, police officers, etc.

Criterion B: Presence of one (or more) intrusive symptoms associated with the traumatic event(s) after the event(s) occurred:

- Recurrent distressing memories
- Recurring nightmares
- Flashbacks, or dissociative reactions in which the person feels the trauma repeating
- Intense or prolonged psychological distress in the face of reminders
- Physical reactions in the face of reminders

Criterion C: Avoidance of stimuli associated with the trauma, as evidence by one or more of the following:

- Avoidance of distressing memories and thoughts about the trauma
- Avoidance of distressing external reminders of the trauma, like people, places, conversations, and activities

Criterion D: Negative alterations to mood and cognition, as evidenced by two (or more) of the following:

- Inability to remember important aspects of the trauma
- Exaggerated negative thoughts about oneself, others, or the world
- Blaming oneself or others for the trauma
- Persistence negative emotional state, like fear, horror, anger, guilt, or shame
- Diminished interest in activities
- Feelings of detachment or estrangement from others
- Inability to experience positive emotions

Criterion E: Alterations in arousal and reactivity, as evidenced by two or more of the following:

- Irritability and angry outbursts with little or no provocation
- Reckless and self-destructive behavior
- Hypervigilance
- Exaggerated startle response
- Problems with concentration
- Difficulty sleeping

Criterion F: Duration of the disturbance is more than 1 month.

Criterion G: The disturbance causes significant distress or impairment in social, occupational, and other important areas of functioning.

Criterion H: Symptoms are not due to medication, substance use, or another medical condition.

Prior to the DSM-5, reactive attachment disorder was included under the category of childhood disorders, while posttraumatic stress disorder was considered an anxiety disorder.

Prior to the DSM-5, the criteria for a diagnosis of reactive attachment disorder were very different from the criteria used in assessment or categorization of attachment styles, such as insecure or disorganized attachment.

There was a lack of clarity about the presentation of the disorder beyond the age of five.[16]

Children with reactive attachment disorder are presumed to have grossly disturbed internal working models of relationships that may lead to interpersonal and behavioral difficulties in later life.

The opening of orphanages in Eastern Europe, following the end of the Cold War in the early 1990s, provided opportunities for research on infants and toddlers brought up in very deprived conditions. Such research broadened the understanding of the prevalence, causes, mechanism, and assessment of disorders of attachment.

---

16   Ibid.

Mr. L's earlier years of upbringing environment seemed to be very similar to other orphanages (see figure 14). Because a variety of clinical phenotypes that are consistent with posttraumatic stress disorder diagnostic criteria, it could no longer simply be considered an anxiety disorder but rather a spectrum with wide array of symptoms cluster with anxiety being just one of its cluster.

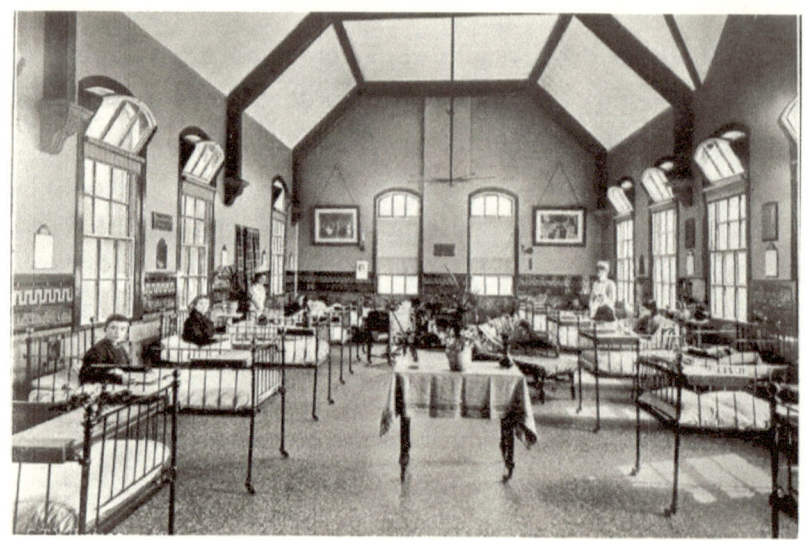

Fig. 14. Illustration of an orphanage sleeping quarter

In the DSM-5, posttraumatic stress disorder serves as the cornerstone of a new definition of trauma that is more explicit and with its symptomatic profile expanded from a three- to four-factor structure without the requirement of subjective responses following traumatic events.[17]According to the DSM-5 classification, Mr. L also met the separate diagnostic criteria for preschool posttraumatic stress disorder diagnosis for children six years old and younger.[18]

17   Neil W. Boris, Charles H. Zeanah, *Work Group on Quality Issues, Practice Parameter for the Assessment and Treatment of Children and Adolescents with Reactive Attachment Disorder of Infancy and Early Childhood, Journal of the American Academy of Child and Adolescent Psychiatry* (2005), 44(11): 1206–1219.

18   American Psychiatric Association, *Diagnostic and Statistical Manual of Mental*

The DSM-5 is considered as one of the most comprehensive and critical resource for clinical practice available for today's mental health clinicians and researchers of all orientations. The information contained in the manual is also valuable to other physicians and health professionals including psychologists, counselors, nurses, and occupational and rehabilitation therapists, as well as social workers and forensic and legal specialists. Despite the wealth and depth of its content, the DSM-5 is often underused and underestimated by skeptics as a source of commentary and context for the disorders whose boundaries it defines. A revised text edition (DSM-5-TR) was released by the American Psychiatric Association Publishing on March 18, 2022.

A Correlation: Reactive Attachment and Posttraumatic Stress

Children with reactive attachment disorder may have a listless appearance. They may seem sad without any discernable reason for being sad. Listlessness might include a lack of reaction to outside stimuli, a lack of interest in the world around them, and a general lack of attachment. They might not smile, even when caregivers try to engage them in fun activities. These are all signs an infant or young child is failing to relate to the world in an emotionally healthy way. A child with reactive attachment disorder might not seek support, even in situations where they need it. Preschool teachers and parents might notice children with this condition don't reach out for assistance or help, even when it's needed, such as to get objects down from high places or help with homework. This can be attributed to an early failure to meet all of the child's emotional and support needs. If a child is not receiving the nurture and support they need in their environment, they will learn not to seek it out.

Disorders, Fifth edition (Arlington, Virginia: 2013), 265–268 and 271–280.

The self-report dimensions of adult reactive attachment disorder may be characterized as insecure, dismissing, preoccupied, or fearful, and they could mediate or precipitate posttraumatic stress disorder. Correlational analyses revealed a significant positive relationship between negative view of self and posttraumatic stress symptomatology but not between negative view of other and posttraumatic stress symptomatology. Regression analyses indicated that having a negative view of self was most highly associated with posttraumatic stress symptoms, followed by a history of physical abuse. The regression analysis further indicated that negative view of other was unrelated to posttraumatic stress symptoms.

Mr. L then resumed speaking in French, confirming that he was severely traumatized by living in a crowded orphanage and he was thankful to be transferred to a Carmelites orphanage where he met Soeur Marie.

CHAPTER5

THE CARMELITES ORDER OF NUNS AND THE PRIMARY EMOTIONS

The History of the Carmelites Order

The order of Carmelites has its origins on Mount Carmel in Palestine, where the prophet Elijah defended the true faith in the God of Israel and where he won the challenge against the priests of Baal. It was also on Mount Carmel that the prophet Elijah, while praying in solitude, saw the small cloud, which brought life-giving rain after a very long drought. From time immemorial, this mountain was considered the lush garden of Palestine and symbol of fertility and beauty. Indeed, Carmel means "garden."

In the twelfth century, following the third crusade, 1189–1191, some penitent pilgrims, who had come from Europe, came together near the Spring of Elijah, in one of the narrow valleys of Mount Carmel, to live out their Christianity as hermits after the example of the prophet Elijah. Although in later times, the Carmelites did not acknowledge anyone in particular as their founder, they remained faithful followers of Elijah while developing a sense of belonging to the Virgin Mary as their patroness, and they became known by her name as Brothers of the Blessed Virgin Mary of Mount Carmel.

The Carmelites inherited a burning passion for the living and true God and the desire to make his Word intimately their own in order to witness to its presence in the world. They became committed to live "in the footsteps of Jesus Christ," with the same intimate and deep feelings which were Mary's.

In order to have some juridical stability, this group of Carmelites or lay hermits turned to the Patriarch of Jerusalem, Albert Avogadro, who lived from 1150 to 1214 and who was then living at St. John of Acre near Mount Carmel, who wrote for them a formula of life. Successive approvals of this formula of life by various popes helped the process of transforming the group into a religious order—a fact which took place at the time of the definitive approval of the text as a rule by Pope Innocent IV in 1247. Thus, the Carmelite Order took its place alongside the Mendicant orders.

However, about 1235, the Carmelites were forced to abandon their place of origin due to the incursions and persecutions of the Saracen Arabs and Muslims who reconquered the Holy Land from the crusaders. Most of them then went back to their country of origin in Europe. Ultimately, they increased and flourished in the sciences and in holiness.

Later, some devoted women joined the monasteries of the friars and, in 1452, became cloistered nuns living in their own communities, which were later reformed. One of the most famous reform started in Spain by Sister Maria Teresa of Jesus, who was born in Montevarchi, Italy, on May 15, 1825, and died on November 14, 1889. From childhood, she had a marked tendency toward prayer and was profoundly connected to Carmelite spirituality from her reading of St. Mary Magdalene de' Pazzi. She also had a great devotion to the Virgin Mary, whom she called my dear mother. The spirit of contemplation, total abandonment to the will of God, and deep union with the Lord were the characteristics of her spiritual life. She felt the irresistible call of the Lord and in spite of many obstacles, she overcame them and fulfilled her calling to become a Carmelite sister.

At the dawn of the French Revolution, the Carmelite Order was established throughout the world with fifty-four provinces. Also as a result of the French Revolution, the order suffered great losses such that, at the end of the 19th century, it was reduced to eight provinces.

Since the time of the Second Vatican Council, between 1962 and 1965, the Carmelites have reflected at length on their identity and on what is fundamental in their lives—namely, "to live a life of allegiance to Jesus Christ and serve him faithfully with a pure heart and a good conscience," in living in fraternity and service, "diakonia," in the midst of the people. They see all this in the lives of the prophet Elijah and the Virgin Mary, who were led by the Spirit of God.

At present, the Carmelite Order (the friars) is formed of provinces, general commissariats, general delegations, hermetical communities, and affiliated communities that are found in all the continents.

On December 2, 2003, in the presence of the pope, the heroic virtue of the Servant of God Maria Teresa of Jesus, also known as Maria Scrilli, was declared, and on Sunday, October 8, 2006, Mother Maria Teresa Scrilli was beatified in Fiesole, Italy.

The Carmelite Order's Charism and Education Style

One of the particular charisms (see figure 15) of the Catholic Carmelite nuns is education. The word charism illustrates special characteristics and values in addition to an overall spiritual orientation. Charism is from the Greek χαρίσμα, which denotes "the grace that God gifts to an individual or group to perform a specific mission in the Church and the world."The Carmelite order believes that the heart of their way of life is contemplation, which is described as "the inflowing of God's grace into a human being" or simply as a "friendship with God," with its charism: "to know and love God, and to make God known and loved."

Fig. 15. The Carmelite Order's charism

At its heart, God's grace and friendship is offered to all people, not as something that can be earned or attained by a person's own efforts but as a free gift of God, given whenever and to whoever God wishes to become contemplative, Carmelites seek to open their hearts to God, practicing the Latin expression "Vacare Deo" (i.e., "Space for God" or "Openness to God").

Prayer, community, and service are the three main elements

that are at the heart of Carmelites charism (see figure 16). In prayer, a friendship is built up with the God, who we know loves his creation. In community building, God is encountered in others who comfort and challenge us. In service, humanity opens its heart to be God's hands in the world, responding to the needs of others, especially the poor, the needy, and the disfranchised.

Fig. 16. Nuns of the Catholic Carmelite Order during a candlelight service

Mr. L then exclaimed with a deep tone of voice that he witnessed and experienced these three elements of the Carmelite Order charism as practiced and exemplified day in, day out by Soeur Marie. And to my surprise, he recited the Carmelites pledge.

As Carmelites, we live our life of allegiance to Jesus Christ and to serve him faithfully with a pure heart and a clear conscience through a commitment to seek the face of the living God (the contemplative dimension of life), through prayer, through fraternity, and through service (diakonia). These three fundamental elements of the charism are not distinct and unrelated values but closely interwoven. All of these we live under the protection, inspiration, and guidance of Mary, Our Lady of Mount Carmel, whom we honor as "our Mother and sister."

Soeur Marie, a Special Carmelites Order Nun

Mr. L was firmly convinced that his destiny changed when he was six years old, as a consequence of his transfer from the state-run orphanage to a Catholic Carmelite order orphanage that was run by nuns.

In the first few months of his stay in that orphanage, several nuns commented on Mr. L's unmatched ability of memorizing poems, children stories, and the Mass in Latin as taught by the Carmelite order of *Ordo Fratrum Beatæ Virginis Mariæ de Monte Carmelo.*[19]He described a tiny, petite, and short nun, Soeur Marie, who was kind and caring and would often ask him if he realizes how detached he was and then, without reservation, called him in French, "Mon chér petit garçon," which he later understood has its English meaning as "my dear little boy."

He became curious about Soeur Marie's language. She told him it was French, he asked if she would teach him to learn it, she agreed and over a period of four months he learned it with perfect fluency. She gave him books to read as a reward for changing his detached behaviors and some of the books he read were from her own collection of classic literature. She also asked him to write essays about the various books he read and the emotions they evoked. He was surprised to experience feelings that he could not describe in words and Soeur Marie helped him elaborate and naming these feelings which included fear, sadness, guilt and happiness the newly felt emotions were different from his only familiar primary emotions of resentment and anger.

---

19   Krmpotic, MD, *Dalmatia, Catholic Encyclopedia* (1908) retrieved 2008.

Anger, the Iceberg of Underlying Emotional Reactions

Anger is an emotion that is expressed to protect or mask other vulnerable feelings. So in his prior orphanage environment, when Mr. L felt intensely afraid, attacked, offended, disrespected, forced, trapped, or pressured, he became angry toward self and others—as if his anger was like an iceberg in that only some of his emotions were visible. His other emotions existed below the waterline, where they were not immediately obvious to his outside observers (see figure 17). Growing up in the deprived orphanage environment, whenever he attempted to suppress his anger, other intolerable feelings were created, which he did not know how to label, but as he learned from Soeur Marie, he was then able to describe them as resentment, bitterness, hostility, hatred, and, in some unbearable events, as overpowering, irresistible rage. When he felt anger, he felt out of control, irrational, unenlightened, uncivilized, and this frequently led to fear, shame, anxiety, and more suppression—a never- ending vicious cycle of emotional turmoil.

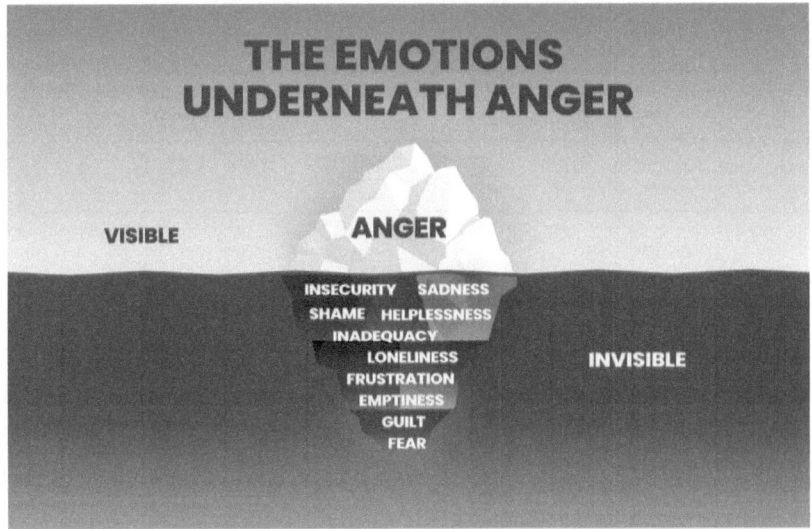

Fig. 17. Anger, the iceberg of underlying emotional reactions

The Newly Felt Primary Emotions

Throughout development and as the brain matures, primary emotions begin to develop and are expressed in response to specific circumstance throughout every person's life span. There are eight primary emotions, and these are anger, sadness, fear, joy, interest, surprise, disgust, and shame. Each one of these eight primary emotions can encompass a spectrum of secondary emotions, as illustrated in table 3.

Table 3. The eight primary emotions with their corresponding secondary emotions

Primary Emotions	Secondary Emotional Expressions
Anger	Fury, outrage, wrath, irritability, hostility, resentment, violence
Sadness	Grief, sorrow, gloom, melancholy, despair, loneliness, depression
Fear	Anxiety, apprehension, nervousness, dread, fright, panic
Joy	Enjoyment, happiness, relief, bliss, delight, pride, thrill, ecstasy
Interest	Acceptance, friendliness, trust, kindness, affection, love, devotion
Surprise	Shock, astonishment, amazement, astoundment, wonder
Disgust	Contempt, disdain, scorn, aversion, distaste, revulsion
Shame	Guilt, embarrassment, chagrin, remorse, regret, contrition

Mr. L was surprised and enlightened whenever he felt any of the primary emotions and some of their secondary expressions as if he had an emotional rebirth with Soeur Marie's never-ending streams of love, care, and encouragement. Her tender mercy and compassion surrounded every second of every minute of every hour of every day of every month of his waking and living moments.

The Development of the Eight Primary Emotions

The concept of basic or primary emotions may have dated back to *the Book of Rites*, a first-century Chinese encyclopedia, which described the seven feelings of joy, anger, sadness, fear, love, disliking, and liking. In the twentieth century, Paul Ekman, who is considered a pioneer in the study of emotions and their relation to facial expressions, identified the six basic emotions of anger, disgust, fear, happiness, sadness, and surprise.[20] He also created an atlas of emotions with more than 10,000 facial expressions and gained a reputation as the best human lie detector in the world.

In the same period of time, Robert Plutchik proposed an innovative theory of the eight basic emotions, which are anger, fear, sadness, disgust, surprise, anticipation, trust, and joy.[21] He also clarified that the primacy of these emotions makes each one triggers behaviors with high survival value, such as the way fear inspires the fight-or-flight response. He also created a wheel of emotions, which is used to illustrate different emotions in a compelling and nuanced way (see figure 18).

---

20   Paul Ekman, Wallace V. Friesman, *Unmasking the Face: A Guide to Recognizing Emotions from Facial Expressions* (Los Altos, California: Malor Books, 2003)

21   Robert Plutchik, *Emotions and Life: Perspectives from Psychology, Biology, and Evolution* (Washington, D.C.: 2002).

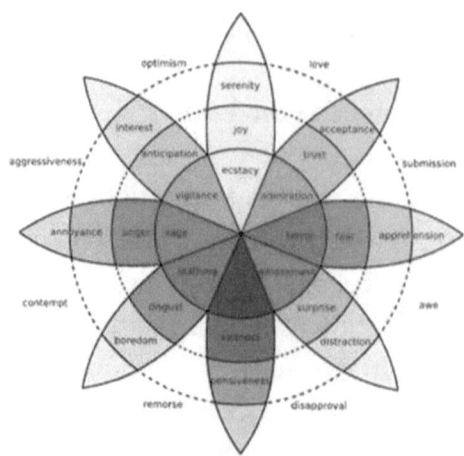

Fig. 18. Illustration of Plutchik's wheel of the basic emotions

I was filled with gratitude and humility while reflecting back on the years of training as a psychiatry resident under the supervision of devoted faculty members of the University of Oklahoma Health Sciences Center, Department of Psychiatry and Behavioral Sciences, Oklahoma College of Medicine in Oklahoma City, Oklahoma, who introduced me to the concept of primary emotions; otherwise, I would have not been able to grasp this component of Mr. L's life's narrative.

CHAPTER6

THE TRAINING OF THE TWENTY-FIRST CENTURY PSYCHIATRIST

The Beginning at Cairo University Faculty of Medicine

Cairo University was initially known as the Egyptian University from 1908 to 1940, was then renamed as King Fouad I University from 1940 to 1952. It was renamed a second time after the Egyptian revolution of 1952. It is Egypt's premier public university with its main campus in the city of Giza, across the Nile from Cairo, Egypt's capital.

The University is one of the fifty largest institutions of higher education in the world, with an enrollment of approximately 155,000 students in twenty-two faculties. Three of Cairo University graduates are Nobel laureates and include the author Naguib Mahfouz, who won the Nobel Prize in Literature in 1988; Yasser Arafat, the former chairman of the Palestine Liberation Organization, who won the Nobel Peace Prize in 1994; and Mohamed ElBaradei, the former director general of the International Atomic Energy Agency, who won the Nobel Peace Prize in 2005.

Some of Cairo University's notable graduates include Boutros Boutros-Ghali, the sixth secretary-general of the United Nations (UN) 1992–1996. It is the second oldest institution of higher education in Egypt after Al-Azhar University, notwithstanding the preexisting higher professional schools that later became constituent colleges of the university. It was founded and funded as the Egyptian University by a committee of private citizens with royal patronage in 1908 and became a state institution under King Fuad I in 1925 (see figure 19).[22]

Fig. 19. Main Entrance to Cairo University campus

In 1940, four years following his death, the university was renamed King Fuad I University in his honor. The faculty of medicine's six-year curriculum is divided into a preparatory preliminary science-focused year at the faculty of sciences, followed by five years of medical education at the faculty of medicine. The first three years of medical education are devoted to basic sciences, followed by the fourth and fifth clinical years; during which, the majority of teaching is delivered in hospital settings.

It was during my fourth year of medical school that I met the cherished and beloved professor of psychiatry, Dr. Mohammed Shaalan (see figure 20), who introduced psychiatry as an artful branch of medicine that combine history, science, and spirituality to reach the depth of the suffering human soul. In addition to conducting group

22   Reid, Donald M. Cairo University and the Making of Modern Egypt. Cambridge: Cambridge UP, 1990. Print. 23.

psychotherapy sessions, Dr. Shaalan practiced and demonstrated the value of psychodrama in eliciting psychopathology and in devising appropriate treatment interventions. He also inaugurated the Mohammed Shaalan Mental Health Center at Forty-four El Kasr El Ainy Street in Cairo to train medical students and psychiatry residents in practicing the art of psychotherapy and psychodrama. Many of the medical students who attended psychodrama sessions also established a collegiate bond and friendship beyond classroom attendance. They attended classical music performances, joined a movie club-discussion group, explored Egyptian antiquity sites, participated in political debates, visited art galleries, and camped on the coast near Alexandria (see figure 21). To honor the invaluable impact of these friends on understanding Mr. L's interconnection to arts and literature, I wish to acknowledge some by mentioning their names: Alyaa, Mervat, Nadia, Salah, Emad, Gerhard, Fayez, Nagui, Wagih, and Essam. To pay tribute to the ones who departed our earthly existence Fouad, Reda, Ismail and Mounir. To recognize others who could not attend the Alexandria camp and still played important roles in the growth of our circle of friends Samih, Nashaat (Nash), Basem, Mona, Sabry, Iman, Amr, Aida, Badawi, and Nader.

Fig. 20. Dr. Mohammed Shaalan

Fig. 21. Packing up following Alexandria coast camping
experience

Dr.Tarek Ali Hassan,professor of medicine and chief of endocrinology at Al-Azhar University in Cairo, was also a composer, musician, writer, painter, and philosopher. His music in a modern polyphonic style has been performed in Egypt and in many countries. He played a pivotal role in demonstrating the integration of cultural norms into the humane practice of medicine. Dr.Yehia El-Rakhawy, professor of psychiatry in Cairo University, was the cofounder of group psychotherapy in Egypt. He introduced the theory of Biorhythmic Evolutionary Psychiatry and directed our attention to the professional and cultural values that would shape our future and "path of thought."

Psychodrama and Mr. L's Existential Conflicts

Dr. Jacob Levy Moreno, the twentieth century psychiatrist (1889–1974), developed psychodrama in the early 1900s, holding its first session in 1921. This therapeutic approach was based on the recognition of the importance of a group encounter to therapy. In addition, Dr. Moreno had combined interests in philosophy, theater, and mysticism.

In the late 1930s, he founded the Beacon Hospital, which featured a therapeutic theater where psychodrama could be practiced as part of therapy, and in 1942, he also established the American Society of Group Psychotherapy.

During a typical psychodrama session, which usually last about ninety minutes, a number of group members gather together. One of the group members is chosen to be the protagonist, and the group leader, also known as the director, calls on the other group members to assist the protagonist's performance—act out a number of scenes in order to allow the work through certain scenarios. Although this acting performance is beneficial for the protagonist, it is also helpful to the other group members, allowing them to assume the role of another person and apply that experience to their own life. The focus during the session is on the acting out of different scenarios, rather than simply talking through them. All of the different elements of the session, including its theatrical staging, props, and lighting, are used to heighten the reality of the scene, either by portraying other characters or by utilizing mirroring, doubling, or role reversal.

During mirroring, the protagonist is first asked to act out an experience. After this, the protagonist steps out of the scene and watch as another actor steps into their role and portrays them in the scene. This followed by doubling, where the double brings to consciousness any thoughts or feelings that another person is unable to express, whether it is because of shyness, guilt, inhibition, politeness, fear, anger, or other primary emotions. In many cases, the person is unaware of these thoughts or, at least, is unable to form the words to express how they are feeling. Therefore, the double attempts to make conscious and give form to the unconscious and/ or under expressed material. The person being doubled has the full right to disown any of the double's statements and to correct them as necessary. In this way, doubling itself can never be wrong. In role reversal, a group member is asked to portray another person while a second actor portrays that group member in the particular scene. This not only prompts the group member to think as the other person but also has some of the benefits of mirroring, as that group member sees him or herself as portrayed by the second actor.

While listening to Mr. L, I suddenly vividly remembered a psychodrama group session where Dr. Shaalan, as the group director, skillfully facilitated one of the group members acting how he felt when he was raised as a child in an orphanage where other orphans bullied him and deprived him on many instances from getting his rations of breakfast food. By acting out his unexpressed feelings of anger, resentment, rage, and fear, he was able to move on and to be liberated from the hurtful feelings, which he has been relieving in his present life. My exposure to the psychodrama process provided me with an asset to understand Mr. L's existential conflicts that were unresolved from childhood and accompanied him throughout his adult life and possibly during other painful traumatic events.

Psychodrama as Therapeutic Intervention

Psychodrama could have specific clinical application for those who are suffering from dysfunctional attachments. I felt inner peace thinking that Mr. L may have indirectly mirrored Soeur Marie when he made the conscious effort to master her spoken French language, which allowed him to emotionally express himself and compensate for the enduring suffering in his earlier years of living in the orphanage. For this reason, psychodrama was often introduced in the treatment of children who have suffered emotional trauma and abuse.

By using role-play and storytelling, children may be able to express themselves emotionally and reveal truths about their experiences, which they are not able to openly discuss with others. Dr. Moreno's theory of child development offered further insight into psychodrama and children, and he suggested that child development could be divided into three stages, beginning with finding personal identity, identifying oneself through the mirror stage, and then ending by recognizing the other person through the role-reversal stage.

Later on, Mr. L listened to the description of Dr. Shaalan's psychodrama approach and, with certainty, accepted its potential benefits. He wished it would have been introduced as a possible intervention during his early stages of emotional development. He then said,

"No regrets!"

An Eclectic Approach to Psychiatry Training

The trend toward the re-medicalization in psychiatry became apparent in the '80s and '90s. Since then, the training of psychiatrists have been empathizing the importance of pharmacological treatment, with fewer training programs offering specialized psychodynamic psychiatry and exposure to the psychoanalytic approach of mental disorders.

I was fortunate and blessed to complete the psychiatry training at the University of Oklahoma Health Sciences Center with the Department of Psychiatry and Behavioral Sciences, Oklahoma College of Medicine in Oklahoma City, Oklahoma (see figure 22). All through the four years of training, I was exposed to, instructed, and supervised by a diverse, and eclectic faculty members. These dedicated psychiatrists and superb clinicians provided numerous opportunities to gain proficiency in an array of clinical modalities, therapeutic and assessment techniques, while serving a population that encompasses a broad variety of ages, psychiatric diagnoses, and levels of functioning within a context of culturally sensitive practice.

Fig. 22. University of Oklahoma Health Sciences Center

This psychiatry training program offered me the opportunity to practice psychiatry with a broad and eclectic approach, which allowed me to experience firsthand the importance of psychoanalysis and psychodynamic psychiatry. The combination of diverse populations, training facilities, and faculty allowed me to gain a deep appreciation of the uniqueness of each individual's emotions and unresolved psychological conflicts. By relying on the tenants of my eclectic training, I attempted to come to grasp with the uniqueness of Mr. L's inner soul.

Psychodynamic Psychotherapy

In this type of therapy, the focus is on the person's relationship with the external world, rather than the relationship with the psychiatrist as in the context of psychoanalysis. It's usually used to treat depression and other serious psychological disorders, especially in those who have lost meaning in their lives and have difficulty forming or maintaining personal relationships. The person is encouraged to speak freely about anything that comes to mind, including current issues, fears, desires, dreams, and fantasies.

The goal is to experience a remission of symptoms but also derive such benefits as increased self-esteem, better use of own talents and abilities, and an improved capacity for developing and maintaining more satisfying relationships.

The theories and techniques that distinguish psychodynamic therapy from other types of therapy include a focus on recognizing, acknowledging, understanding, expressing, and overcoming negative and contradictory feelings and repressed emotions in order to improve the interpersonal experiences and relationships. This includes promoting the understanding of the role that repressed earlier emotions play in affecting current decision-making, behavior, and relationships.

Psychodynamic therapy also aims to help those who are aware of and understand the origins of their social difficulties but are not able to overcome their problems on their own. Patients learn to analyze and resolve their current issues and change their behavior in current relationships through this deep exploration and analysis of earlier experiences and emotions.

One of the influential mentors/teachers/educators at the University of Oklahoma Health Sciences Center, with the Department of Psychiatry and Behavioral Sciences, was Dr. Gordon H. Deckert (see figure 23), who taught me and my class of psychiatry residents the pearls of psychodynamic psychiatry, which emphasize the centrality of intrapsychic and unconscious conflicts in the development of internal psychic defenses to avoid unpleasant consequences of conflict, especially from early childhood experiences. The underlying life issues and dynamics will reemerge in the context of the relationship with the therapist and expressed in the form of the defense mechanisms of transference, countertransference, and resistance. Using of free association is usually the road that explores internal conflicts and focusing on interpretations of transference, defense mechanisms, and current symptoms would enhance working through the presenting problems. In addition, psychodynamic psychotherapy trusts in insight as a critically important element of successful therapy.

Fig. 23. Dr. Gordon H. Deckert

Dr. Phebe Tucker, the vice chair of education and professor of psychiatry in her eulogy, eloquently mentioned that Dr. Deckert was named the Medical Czar of Oklahoma in 1957 and was tasked with designing protocols in the event of nuclear war. Awards have been named after him and bestowed upon him, and despite the notoriety he has earned, he felt that his most important contribution in teaching physicians was understanding the person when diagnosing an illness and treating the person, not the disease, as the most effective way of treating a disease.

He was born in South Dakota on May 18, 1930, and died at the age of ninety on June 10, 2020. His spirit lives on in the memories of the many physicians he taught and entertained but will also be felt by future physicians. He enriched medical education and medical practices by empathizing the human side of the doctor-patient relationship. I was overwhelmed with thankfulness, knowing that Dr. Deckert's psychodynamic training influenced and guided my intervention in understanding Mr. L's plights and childhood unsolved conflicts.

Psychiatry, a Humane Discipline

One of the inspiring mentors, who later became my supervisor when I worked at the Oklahoma VA Medical center, is Dr. Charles E. Smith, who was born on March 5, 1927, in Shawnee and departed this life to be with his Lord on January 17, 2001, after a valiant battle with cancer.

Dr. Smith served as a lieutenant in the US Army in 1945–1947. He earned his bachelor's degree in 1950 at Oklahoma City University and his medical degree in 1954 at the University of Oklahoma. Dr. Smith organized the second professional corporation (Professional Corporation of Psychiatry) to be incorporated in the State of Oklahoma in 1961. He served as part-time staff physician at the VA Medical Center (1958–1973), as chief of mental health services (1973–1983), and as chief of staff (1983–1988). He was active as a professor in the Department of Psychiatry and Behavioral Sciences at the University of Oklahoma Health Sciences Center. He served as the courtesy staff at Presbyterian, Oklahoma Memorial, and McBride bone and joint hospitals and as active staff at St. Anthony and Integris Baptist Medical Center. He was actively involved in many community, state, and national medical associations and enjoyed a strong national recognition in the field of psychiatry. He served as treasurer of the American College of Psychiatry for nine years. He was the Oklahoma representative to the American Psychiatric Association for fifteen years. He served on the boards of the Oklahoma State Department of Mental Health and Mental Health Association in Oklahoma County for many years. He received the Martin Luther King Award from the Black Affairs Committee at the VA Medical Center, and the primary conference room of the Oklahoma City VA Medical Center was dedicated in his honor.

Dr. Smith, along with his team of devoted clinicians: Drs. Gloria B. Green, Joseph B. Ruffin, Jenny Boyer, and so many other supportive staff and supervisors, instilled valuable time-honored principles in those whom he trained and prepared as future psychiatrists. These principles were based on the values of loving and caring for psychiatric patients the same way one would care for orphans and society-disfranchised and neglected human souls.

Dr. Smith left me with the legacy of psychiatry as the ultimate humanistic branch of practicing medicine. His priceless influence became an important element of my attempt to build a personal connection with Mr. L.

Mental Health, the Global View

Dr. Jean E. Carlin (see figure 24) was born in Hibbing, Minnesota, on July 24, 1930. As a child, she lived in many cities until her father's death in 1937. Her mother returned to Minnesota after her husband's passing to raise Jean and her younger sister, Joan. She grew up to be quite a scholar, earning an MD and PHD from the University of Minnesota. She went on to teach psychology at North Park College, Illinois; opened a family practice in Long Beach, California; became a teacher and a dean at the University California, Irvine School of Medicine; went on many medical missions to Vietnam during the Vietnam War and offered her medical and psychiatric expertise to heal the South Vietnamese people who were traumatized by the Vietnam War. She also served in the National Guard. She became the director of the psychiatry residency training program at the University of Oklahoma Health Sciences Center, Department of Psychiatry and Behavioral Sciences from 1983–1986, and had a global approach to the training of psychiatry residents. She encouraged each new class of residents to be involved in study, research, and practice of improving mental health for all people from all cultural backgrounds and worldwide. She took into consideration disparities in mental health treatment and care across cultures and countries. She offered elective culture seminars that touched on various topics, including developing cultural competencies, learning how to provide service delivery in limited resource settings, understanding epidemiology in cultural and geographic contexts, learning how to navigate health systems and policies, and finding ways to improve access to care and treatment.

Fig. 24. Dr. Jean E. Carlin

A global approach to mental illness required the psychiatry residents to meet several core competencies, such as:

- accepting responsibility and following through with difficult tasks,
- practicing within the scope of own abilities and parameters of the local institution,
- responding to patients' unique characteristics and needs,
- demonstrating integrity and ethical behavior,
- demonstrating receptiveness to instruction by local and nonlocal providers, and

- developing a personal system for stress reduction and coping mechanisms for inevitable tragic medical events that will be encountered in different cultural settings.

Dr. Carlin passed the baton of directing the psychiatry residency training program to Dr. Blaine Shaffer, and they both contributed to the training and clinical growth of many of my colleagues who went on and pursued successful careers as mental health professionals and practicing psychiatrists in private, community, and academic settings, such as Drs. Richard Luc, Pamela Hamilton, Mary Olowin, Stephen Hopper, Deanna Storts, Jimmy Lowery, Phuong Tran, Evelyn Miller, Twyla Smith, David Linden, Gayathri Dasharathy, Samuel Lensgraf, Heather Geis, Emily McLean, E. Michael Smith, David Calenzani, Venkatesh Bhat, and Phebe Tucker Dr. Carlin passed away peacefully at her home in Seal Beach, California, on June 6, 2017. Her influence remains a guiding light in my daily attempts to approach mental illness from a global perspective, as revealed in Mr. L's yearning of being understood.

Consciousness, Spirituality, and Culture

The establishment of a local medical school program had been a long- standing interest in the San Joaquin Central Valley of California—a geographic location where a shortage of physicians, special needs in rural health services, and limited access to continuing professional education were daunting challenges. After several earlier attempts to attract a medical school to the valley, interest and efforts revived when a 1970 report by the Carnegie Commission of Higher Education and the Nation's Health identified Fresno as a desirable site for a health science center. the feasibility of a permanent medical education program in Central Valley was explored in a report prepared under the auspices of the consortium with the help of grant funds from the city and county of Fresno. The report was persuasive and resulted in the university's decision to plan a permanent clinical branch in the valley with responsibility assigned to the UCSF campus. In 1975, the California State Legislature gave assurance of continued support of the program and the Veterans Administration (VA) provided a seven- year grant of more than $10 million to sup- port the program. The VA also provided $3.1 million to meet the medical building's construction costs. With that, UCSF-Fresno medical education program was inaugurated. Since then, the program has grown in size and scope and plays an essential role in answering the health-care needs of California's Central Valley. The UCSF School of Medicine-Fresno branch campus is housed in a state-of-the-art center located at 155 N. Fresno Street, adjacent to Community Regional Medical Center in downtown Fresno. When it opened in 2005, the three-story, 82,000-square-foot UCSF-Fresno facility consolidated the various residency programs and administrative staff together under one roof for the first time since

UCSF-Fresno was established in 1975. Since then, the UCSF-Fresno health sciences center has been serving as a hub for medical education and research in California's San Joaquin Valley. The high-tech facility (see figure 25) features a multimedia auditorium, advanced audio and visual-supported conference rooms with full teleconferencing services, a digital medical research library, clinical skills lab with high-fidelity simulation equipment and digital-recording capabilities, and an outdoor amphitheater. In addition, UCSF-Fresno includes a clinical research center and staff who oversee the operation of faculty-led clinical trials and other research that addresses health issues specific to the valley. Dr. Robert Hierholzer, the chief of Psychiatry, at the Fresno VA Central California Health Care System and a clinical professor of psychiatry is a dynamic teacher with keen interests in cross-cultural, geriatric psychiatry and an expert in Institutional Review Boards recruited me to join the Fresno VA and subsequently I became a faculty member of the UCSF-Fresno Medical Education Program. As a faculty member of the UCSF-Fresno Department of Psychiatry, I participated in meetings and seminars that were planned and directed under the leadership of the esteemed colleague Dr. Avak A. Howsepian, who advanced state- of-the-art heated debates on the values of integrating consciousness, spirituality, and culture in the overall assessment and treatment of patients. In addition to Drs. Howsepian and Hierholzer, other UCSF Department of Psychiatry faculty members including Drs. Scott Ahles, Craig Campbell, Hoyle Leigh, Rick Reinfurt, Tirath Gill, Doris Tan, Karen Kraus and John Tran and so many other colleagues contributed to my growth in grasping the complexity of the characteristics and key events that compose the essentials of human existence related to birth, growth, emotion, aspiration, conflict, and mortality. Mr. L's responses during our initial encounter enlightened me and reminded me of the many perspectives of anthropology, art, biology, history, literature, philosophy, psychology, and religion. He helped me in rekindling my unparallel recognition to all of the UCSF Department of Psychiatry colleagues along with their administrating staff members, Ms. Kathleen Perkins, Ms. Barbara Price, Ms. Leslie Irion, Ms. Inez Sweazy and Ms. Lisa Gonzales.

Fig. 25. UCSF Fresno Health Sciences Center Building

The Chemical Dependency Treatment Program

The VA Central California Health Care System (VACCHCS) is located in Fresno, California. It is a general medical and surgical center with state-of-the-art primary, secondary, and tertiary care in major diagnostic and treatment specializations, including psychiatric and mental health services. Under the leadership of Director, Mr. Alan Perry, Associate Director Ms. Susan Shyshka, Chiefs of Staff, Drs. William Cahill and Wessel Meyer, Chief of Quality Assurance Mr. Jack Shantz and Public Affairs officer Mr. David Phillips, the VACCHS has always been committed to fulfilling President Lincoln's promise: "To care for him who shall have borne the battle, and for his widow, and his orphan", by serving and honoring the men and women who are America's Veterans. One of the mental health services provided included the Chemical Dependency treatment Program (CDTP) which was later changed to SUDP, this specialized program provides treatment for substance abuse and addiction. It is a highly-structured outpatient treatment program which is carried out by a team of skilled clinicians, including psychiatrists, psychologists, social workers, counselors, and addiction therapists. The program is also a training site for the psychiatry residents of the UCSF-Fresno Department of Psychiatry. The CDTP emphasizes and supports the development of strategies to achieve a sustained recovery and prevent frequent relapses and the restoration of a productive and an addiction-free lifestyle. During my tenure as the medical director of the CDTP program, I was enriched and introduced to the concept of addiction recovery in my daily encounters with its chief of services, Dr. Kellie Condon; and its clinical staff, Drs. Geoff Twitchell, Tirath Gill, and Roy Raroque; physician assistant, Mr. Leonard Williams, and among so many other providers, Mr. Thomas O'Rourke, Ms. Phyllis Byers, Ms. Sallie Bell, Mr. Aaron Utendahl, Ms. Lynnette Drummond, Mr. Marshall Arteaga, Mr. Antonio Cuyler, Mr. James "Bill" Robinson, Ms. Lora Allen, Mr. Howard Earl, Ms. Marjorie Harp, Mr. Rick Hernandez, Ms. Theresa Stahl, Ms. Delores Terry, Ms. Audrey Houston, Ms. Sharmel Bender, Mr. Tom Williams and Ms. Emma Nichols. The CDTP daily operation was supported by the chief of mental health services, Dr. Nestor Manzano, and the director of the inpatient and emergency psychiatric services, Dr. Dwayne Depry, Dr. Matt Battista Chief of Psychology and Neuropsychology program Lead Chaplain, Terry Rommereim and Voluntary Service Chief, Ms. Mary Golden Placido Suicide Prevention Program Supervisor, Mr. Jerry Silva were an essential asset to CDTP mission. Mental health clinic staff, Drs. Jacob Mathew and Paula Solomon, Mr. Joe Arve, Mr. Rober Emes, Mr. Jeffrey Faye, Mr. Gilbert D'Souza and Ms. Diane Elble provided referral, follow-up and support to veterans admitted to CDTP. Specialized posttraumatic stress disorder treatment was provided by Drs. Tracy Thomas, Elizabeth Mace and Bonny Bronson. Clinical research projects initiated by Drs. Robert Hierholzer and Bita Ghafoori and administrative support provided by Ms. Linda Hayes and the medical assistant Ms. Andrea Willis, Ms. Shealon Hilliard-White and Ms. Pamela Franklin. Although

Mr. L did not suffer from the afflictions of substance abuse and addiction, the experiences that I gained from CDTP provided me with a tool to introduce him to the concept of recovery from childhood and Vietnam War emotional traumas.

Geisel School of Medicine at Dartmouth

This graduate medical school of Dartmouth College is in Hanover, New Hampshire. It is the fourth medical school in the United States and was founded in 1797 by New England physician Nathan Smith. It is one of seven Ivy League medical schools. Several milestones in medical care and research have taken place at Dartmouth, including the introduction of stethoscopes to US medical education, the first clinical x-ray, and the first intensive care unit (ICU) in the United States in 1955. The school has a student body of approximately seven hundred students and more than 2,300 faculty and researchers. Geisel organizes research through over a dozen research centers and institutes, attracting more than $140 million in grants annually, and is ranked as a top medical school by US News and World Report for both primary care and biomedical research. Geisel has numerous clinical partners, including Dartmouth-Hitchcock Medical Center, White River Junction Veterans Administration Medical Center, California Pacific Medical Center, and Manchester Veterans Administration Medical Center.

The Dartmouth-Hitchcock Medical Center is a general medical and surgical teaching hospital. It is a 396-inpatient bed hospital and serves as a major tertiary-care referral site for patients throughout northern New England. As an academic medical center, it offers primary, specialty, and subspecialty care, as well as high-quality education and world-class research in partnership with the Geisel School of Medicine at Dartmouth, as well as the Thayer School of Engineering at Dartmouth and the Dartmouth Institute for Health Policy and Clinical Practice. It is headquartered in Lebanon, New

Hampshire, on a 225-acre campus (see figure 26) in the heart of the Upper Connecticut River Valley and employs more than eight thousand employees. One of its partners is the Live Well/Work Well (LWWW) primary care program. It was created to foster a vision to overcome illness-induced obstacles, fuel motivation, and provide direction to maintain the health, safety, and well-being of patients, staff, and employee. As a consultant psychiatrist, I was a team member of LWWW program. I had the opportunity to share in the mission of this innovative approach of providing mental health and psychiatric intervention within the framework of a comprehensive and an integrated multidisciplinary treatment approach. In the course of my affiliation with Geisel School of Medicine at DartmouthDepartment of Psychiatry from 1992 to 2000 and the LWWW Program in 2015 and 2016, I had the great privilege of witnessing and working with Drs. Alan Green, William C. Torrey, Peter M. Silberfarb, Ronald L. Green, Bradley V. Watts, Heba Gad, Daniel E. O'Donnell, Megan C. Adamson, and Ms. Danielle Basta, APRN. These specialized and clinically skilled providers devoted their professional life to improving the care of patients with severe mental illnesses and integrating psychiatric care within the general frame of primary care.Their comprehensive treatment approach helped me in navigating Mr. L's medical and psychological dispositions.

Fig. 26. The Dartmouth-Hitchcock Medical Center

C H A P T E R 7

LISTENING TO THE MUSIC AND THE LYRICS— INSTRUCTION IN HUNTING AND BASEBALL

Let It Be

Although not included as a component of the Carmelite Order charism, Soeur Marie encouraged several of her pupils to listen to musical compositions and songs. Students who expressed interest in playing music were given lessons by the nuns with musical background using the orphanage classical piano. When a musical instrument was not available, donations were elicited from the surrounding communities through the public library and local stores' billboard advertisements.

One day, a person came to the orphanage to donate a guitar. Up to that time, several children, including Mr. L, had never seen a guitar! They were allowed to touch the instrument, and in the midst of their astonishment, the donor played and sang The Beatles's song *"Let It Be."*[23]

Mr. L became overwhelmed by a mix of emotions of surprise, anticipation, joy, and sadness. He left the happy gathering and run to his bed and was sobbing, and he could not stop crying. Soeur

---

23   *The Beatles, Anthology* (Boston, Massachusetts: Chronicle Books, 2000).

Marie attempted to console him to no avail. The next morning, he apologized to everybody and confined to Soeur Marie that the lyrics of "Let It Be"—

When I find myself in times of trouble Mother Mary comes to me Speaking words of wisdom, let it be. And in my hour of darkness She is standing right in front of me Speaking

words of wisdom, let it be. Let it be, let it be. Whisper words of wisdom, let it be. And when the broken-hearted people Living in the world agree, there will be an answer, let it be. For though they may be parted there is Still a chance that they will see

just pierced his heart because he anticipated that she is Mother Mary and that he will lose her. Soeur Marie reassured him that the concluding lyrics —

And when the night is cloudy, there is still a light that shines on me, shine on until tomorrow, let it be. I wake up to the sound of music Mother Mary comes to me Speaking words of wisdom, let it be. Let it be, let it be. There will be an answer, let it be. Let it be, let it be, Whisper words of wisdom, let it be

are a confirmation that she will always be there when he wakes up every morning. Although he felt reassured, he began to retreat back to the very familiar past feelings of detachment because he could not bear any future possibility of losing Soeur Marie.

The Beatles

The Beatles are one of the most famous and influential English rock bands of all time, formed in 1960. In the first few years, the band members included Pete Best and Stuart Sutcliffe, but ultimately, the band gained fame early in the '60s, with its remaining members, John Lennon, Paul McCartney, Ringo Starr, and George Harrison. The Beatles were also often referred to as the Fab Four (see figure 27) and, by 1964, had reached international stardom, leading the way for British bands to enter and dominate the US pop market in what was called the British Invasion. The band became so famous with their mix of '50s rock, beat, hard rock, psychedelic, pop, and even Indian music and spawned Beatlemania, an intense fan frenzy that, by 1966, made it impossible for them to perform live because of all the screaming fans in the audience.

Fig. 27. The Beatles, the Fab Four during a news conference

The Beatles broke up in 1970 but left their undeniable mark on the music evolution and culture. "Let It Be" is one of The Beatles's many iconic ballads, written and sung by Paul McCartney. It has a level of lyrics repetition suggesting that this song was written quickly and through emotional inspiration. Paul McCartney explained that the song's inspiration was a dream he had with his mother, Mary McCartney, who died of cancer when he was fourteen and that it was great to visit with his mother and that he felt very blessed to have that dream and that his mother had told him, "It will be all right, just let it be."

When asked if the song referred to the Virgin Mary, the mother of Jesus Christ, Paul McCartney typically answered the question by assuring his fans that they can interpret the song however they like. For Mr. L, this song was so close to home, and he vowed to never touch or come near any guitar and to never listen to The Beatles. He clarified that his decision to do so was based on his extensive reading of The Beatles's life as a bonded and unmatched famous band and because "*Let It Be*" was their final single before Paul McCartney announced his departure from the band, which eventually led to The Beatles's breakup.

Although in September 1969, John Lennon, the band's founder, privately informed the other Beatles that he was leaving the group, there was no public acknowledgment of the breakup until Paul McCartney announced on the tenth of April 1970 that he was leaving The Beatles, during the last "*Let It Be*" recording session.
    Mr. L expressed his innermost fears of getting attached to any song that would end with a breakup of its performers.

Destination: London

The Beatles transported my mind back to an earlier phase of my life when I lived in England. In elementary school, I had a geography assignment to present two cities with their unique characteristics to my classmates. I chose San Francisco and London. One of London's historical building was Belgrave Square. I briefly entertained the thought of visiting that site. At the time, it was just a lofty aspiration of a naive student. Following the unexpected passing of my father, Raoul, I had a prolonged period of grief. My mother, Jeannette, was sorting through some of my old notebooks and school assignments, hoping to find some of my earlier happy memories. She found a school report card with a footnote describing my dreams to visit Belgrave Square if I would ever travel to London. I had just graduated from the University of Cairo, Faculty of Medicine. My mother subtly tucked the school report card beneath the leather folder that held my medical degree diploma. While preparing for my internship, I found the report card and remembered that there was a possibility of completing my first year of internship at the Faculty of Medicine of the University of London, affiliated hospitals based on its long-established academic reciprocity with the University of Cairo, Faculty of Medicine. That idea was immediately encouraged and fostered by my mother, who, with a joyful laugh, reminded me that if I pursued that plan, I would have the chance to also see and visit Belgrave Square! Despite the obstacles and logistic hurdles of trying to obtain a visa to visit the UK, my mother's relentless prayers prevailed, and here I was sitting on a flight from Cairo to London. The average flight duration of five hours and twenty minutes seemed to have only lasted for few minutes. I was planning with excitement and anxious anticipation a year-long internship in London's various teaching hospitals.

The Professional and Linguistic Assessments Board

Unbeknown to me earlier that same year, the UK initiated new requirements for overseas physicians to undertake the Professional and Linguistic Assessments Board test or the PLAB test, a two-part written and clinical exam. The test must be taken by overseas medical school graduates to assure their possession of the basic knowledge and skills to practice medicine in the UK. Besides its high cost of one thousand English pounds sterling, it is only administered on certain dates that needed to be reserved far in advance. I realized that my dreams of completing an internship year in London's teaching hospitals could not be realistically achieved. Rather than succumbing to the harshness of this unexpected gloomy news, I decided to stay in London for a year to experience firsthand the hard knocks of life. With a meager change of few English pound's sterling, I was driven to look for a job and a place to stay. Five weeks passed and with few coins remaining in my empty pockets, an irresistible surge of despair emerged which was expressed in blurry teary eyes. I initially attributed it to raindrops smearing my eye glasses. While wiping the raindrops, a glimpse of clear vision ensued pointing toward a job posted on the glass door of a restaurant. Hesitantly with drenched clothes, I ventured into an unknown territory. The manager asked if I needed an umbrella and wondered about my teary eyes. I rested my case and described my dire circumstances. He ordered me a meal and asked me to wait for his boss. An hour later, which seemed like eternity, a gentleman dressed in a shiny three-piece gray suit appeared and introduced himself as Mr. Andy Darko. He is an owner of a chain of Wimpy's Hamburgers. He seemed to have been contemplating the prospect of my becoming one of his employees as a waiter in another Wimpy he owned in the London's suburb of Muswell Hill.

Up and down the Hills of Muswell Hill

Mr. Andy Darko was originally from the Greek section of the island of Cyprus. He was known as a successful business entrepreneur who, over a ten-year span, bought and continued to own fast-food restaurants and Wimpy's Hamburgers in several of London's touristic neighborhoods. One evening, Mr. Darko came to the Muswell Hill Wimpy's Hamburger and asked for his special coffee; the manager on duty was new and did not recognize him as being the owner and questioned him about a special coffee order that was not on the menu. I frantically interrupted the conversation and apologized to Mr. Darko. He invited me to sit and asked me if I would like to be promoted to become a manager of one of his restaurants. I told him that I was planning to return home to complete my internship at Cairo University, Faculty of Medicine teaching Hospitals and to pursue a career in psychiatry. He was surprised that he was never told that I graduated from medical school. He proceeded to tell me that his family fled the island of Cyprus as a consequence of intercommunal violence that erupted between the Greek Cypriots and the Turkish Cypriots in late 1963. He always wanted to be a doctor, and his dreams were dashed because he had to support his family by working menial jobs for a decade before he prospered. He looked at me with a kind stare and pleaded that I get acquainted with the British medical system. He strongly encouraged me to save money and to take the PLAB test and assertively empathized,"You will have an impressive resume if you do your internship in London." He gave me a bicycle to ride up and down the hills of Muswell Hill so as to gain an appreciation of its landscape and its proximity to the greater city of London with its several teaching hospitals.

Muswell Hill is a north London suburban district, which reaches 335 feet above sea level. It is close to many beautiful neighborhoods such as Alexandra Park, Highgate Woods, Fortis Green Road, Charing Cross, Hampstead Garden, East Finchley, and Crouch End. Muswell Hill Broadway and the main shopping streets still maintain their historic Edwardian architecture character, with most of the original facades preserved above street level. With an indescribable thrill, I heeded Mr. Darko's advice and rode the bicycle up and down the hilly roads of Muswell Hill and nearby historic neighborhoods.

The Royal College of Psychiatrists

I usually rode the bicycle in familiar streets, but one day, I ventured into a new neighborhood and was lost. A lady was riding her bicycle close by and waived a flag and signaled me to stop. When I did, she gave me a flyer about a lecture that was going to be given at Belgrave Square. Stunned by this providential coincidence, I lost control of the bike and fell off the curb, superficially cut my left index finger. The lady, Mrs. M, was immensely disturbed and gently admonished my reckless riding. She asked that I promise her to stop riding any bicycle until I am properly re-trained. Mrs. M then gave me a booklet of buses and subway tickets and suggested that I use these modes of transportation if I decide to attend the lecture at Belgrave Square.

The next day, I told Mr. Darko about my misadventure with the bicycle, and he graciously confirmed Mrs. M's admonishment and reclaimed his bicycle. My initial disappointment vanished while riding a bus that was heading toward the delightful realization of my dream of visiting Belgrave Square. I was awed by the architecture of this large nineteenth-century garden square, so I took an instant camera photo of the building to send to my mother, and she later acknowledged its reception with joyful delectation. Mrs. M was one of the main speakers during the lecture presentation. She illustrated the history of Belgrave Square and its current occupants of embassies, charities, and institutes. I thanked her and assured her of my abandonment of bicycle riding. She asked me if I was an architect; I nodded that my brother Hadi is an architect in Toronto, Canada and that he designs unique buildings to suit their existing environments without altering any natural existing landscapes. Astonished by such a concept and with elevated eye brows, she asked, so what do you do? I told her about my aspiration to become a psychiatrist. She smiled and revealed an unexpected surprise that Belgrave Square also housed the offices of the Royal College of Psychiatrists. She also mentioned that the college conducts seminars that provide public information about mental health and psychiatric treatment. I could not believe my ears and garnished some courage to ask if I could attend some of these seminars. Mrs. M seemed perplexed and gave me a laminated card which I could use as a permit for admission to Belgrave Square when it was not opened to the general public. I did not know how to thank her; I gave her the address of the Wimpy's Hamburgers so that I could offer her a special meal as a personal guest. She smiled and wished me well. I could hardly wait for my next day off work at Wimpy. I wanted to come back to Belgrave Square to spend time at the Royal College of Psychiatrists.

On my first stopover, I was asked to briefly describe the purpose of my visit. I was pleasantly surprised when I was told that because I already graduated from medical school, I could attend some of the psychiatric clinical presentations. The Royal College of Psychiatrists is the main professional organization of psychiatrists in the UK and is responsible for training and certifying psychiatrists in the UK. During a subsequent visit, I asked about my prospective of being trained as a psychiatrist in the UK. The answer was short but conclusive. I must pass the PLAB test first, then consider an approximate six years of postgraduate training in psychiatry and taking two required examinations. The PLAB test requirement could be waived if I was able to secure a house officer post in Ireland. In a subsequent visit, the Royal College of Psychiatrists had relocated its offices from Belgrave Square to Prescot Street in London, near Aldgate, and I bade farewell to Belgrave Square.

Ireland Detour—Ferry Crossing—Turbulent Water

Mrs. M accepted my invitation and came one day to Wimpy. Her visit coincided with a surprise appearance of Mr. Darko. Although a little embarrassed, I introduced them based on their mutual knowledge of my bicycle accident. They sat and spent time talking and concocted a plan to get me to Ireland. I applied for junior house officer post in Ireland, and to my surprise, I was invited by the Carlow District Hospital to come for an interview for a general surgery spot, which I was going to assertively decline since my interests were in psychiatry. Mr. Darko forcibly intervened and went ahead and purchased my tickets to get to Ireland and asked his tailor to fit me for a suit to impress my prospective interview committee. He insisted that this was a one in a lifetime chance to complete an internship without taking the PLAB test so that in six years, I would become a Royal College certified psychiatrist. So here I am on a voyage which began with a train ride from London to Liverpool, then embarking a ferry boat to Dublin to board on a bus that promptly arrived at the Carlow District Hospital.

The interviewers challenged my motives in seeking a post in general surgery since my interests are in psychiatry. I agreed with their impression and confirmed that I did not and I could not afford taking the PLAB test and it would be waived if I completed the junior house officer year in their district hospital. I was hoping that they would deny me that post. I could not imagine myself as a surgery house officer. I was asked to wait in the front lobby of the hospital until they reached a decision. Their deliberation was relatively short and lasted seventeen minutes. I was escorted back to a different office where I was asked by an administrator to complete employment and background check forms and was handed a congratulation note signed by the interview committee. My hands were shaking with hesitancy and profuse sweating. A sudden knock on the door interrupted the process. One of the interviewers rushed in and asked if I signed the forms."Not yet,"replied the administrator.Thank goodness! We were all so worried. There was another candidate for the same post; he was delayed on the road. He was Irish and a graduate of the trinity College Dublin School of Medicine; he was more qualified for the post—thank heavens! Here is a voucher for your travel and overnight lodging expenses. Best of luck, you may find a post as junior house officer in psychiatry. Initially shocked but deeply relieved, I looked forward to my return to Muswell Hill. My trip back on the ferry was one of agonized abdominal cramps, headaches, and sea sickness due to turbulent sea waves and high winds, as if nature was confirming that Ireland was not a destination to pursue at that particular phase of life's journey.

An Inescapable Solution

With anxious expectation, I was welcomed by Mr. Darko. He refused to accept the reimbursement voucher and asked me to keep the money so that I can travel to various places prior to my return to Egypt. I continued to work at Wimpy for six more months, and on weekends, I went to various museums, art galleries, attended music concerts, theatrical performances, and walked around in many of London's historical sites. The time has come to gather my belongings and to bid my farewell to Mr. Darko. He reminded me that although I did not complete a year of internship, he believed that my year in London was an enriching real-life experience. I expressed my sincere gratitude to his gracious and generous heart. He said he never say goodbyes but would like me to meet his neighbor's wife, Mrs. J, prior to my boarding the flight back to Egypt which was planned in two days. He added that he promised his neighbor that I would help him with his daily life's crisis. I had an irresistible urge to retreat but contemplated the notion that any helpful intervention would reflect my appreciation toward Mr. Darko's boundless kindness and generosity.

I was introduced to Mrs. J as a future psychiatrist in the making. Mrs. J had history of multiple suicide attempts by alcohol and prescription medications overdose. These attempts were her only solution to escape living with an intolerable guilt that stemmed from a car accident that occurred fifteen years earlier. She was the driver; her sister was in the passenger seat. And Mrs. J fell asleep on the wheel. The car hit a curb; her sister was injured and hospitalized and, as a consequence, had a miscarriage. Although her sister quickly recovered and had three subsequent successful deliveries of healthy and beautiful children, Mrs. J blamed herself for her sister's miscarriage and found suicide as the only possible solution of her mental agony. Due to her past failed suicidal attempts, she was contemplating other means to end her life but would not reveal these means to anyone else. Her husband had to retire early from his successful career as an accountant to constantly assure his wife's well- being and to prevent any future suicide attempts. I quietly prayed to be granted insight and wisdom to steer through an unknown arena. I was facing Mrs. J and realized that we were surrounded by empty bookshelves. I suddenly imagined that the book *Man Against Himself* was standing alone in one of the bookshelves. In this landmark book, the author and psychiatrist, Dr. Karl A Menninger, examined the impulse toward self-destructiveness as a misdirection of the instinct for survival, a turning inward of the aggressive behavior developed for self-preservation. I conveyed Dr. Menninger's insights. There was immutable silence, then Mrs. J stood up, shook my hand, walked out, called her husband, embraced him, and they both cried. She then said, "I want to live."

Mr. Darko was summoned to their house, and a joyful melody was played by Mrs. J. She has not touched her harp for fifteen years. Two days later, he drove me in his Rolls-Royce to Heathrow Airport. I safely boarded the flight back to Cairo, anticipating a year of internship as a junior house officer in various Cairo University, Faculty of Medicine—affiliated teaching hospitals. I reflected back on my year of working at the Wimpy and Mr. Darko's generosity. I was given an imaginable opportunity to travel throughout England, spent three days in Ireland, visited friends in France, spent time with friends and family in Canada, and flew to San Francisco to see and walk on the Golden Gate bridge, as it was described in my elementary school assignment. I shared Mr. Darko's, Mrs. M's, and Mrs. J's life narratives and Dr. Menninger's insights with Mr. L. He reflected especially on Mrs. J's suicide attempts as the only inescapable solution of her guilt. He confirmed that he wished to die but would never attempt suicide. I remained hopeful that he may decide to read Dr. Karl A. Menninger's book, *Man Against Himself.* I am not sure if he ever did.

What Was the Dream All About? A Surprise Birthday Party

On Mr. L thirteenth birthday, which also coincided with Soeur Marie's fortieth birthday, she planned with all the other nuns to hold a surprise birthday party. One of his birthday's gifts was a personal letter from a Second World War (WWII) veteran.

During that interview interval, Mr. L then voluntarily informed me that he was dreaming about this birthday just before he woke up. He described the WWII veteran as a New Hampshire native. His name was Lieutenant John, who owned an antique and a gun shop. He offered him an invitation to learn hunting and to play baseball. Lieutenant John was a widower and a man of few words, who had three grown-up daughters but no sons. He also had seven grandchildren, and none of them were interested in hunting or baseball. He instructed Mr. L on the humanistic laws of hunting and the skillful techniques of playing baseball. The lieutenant fostered Mr.L innate talent, as a left-handed young man, in both hunting and baseball. As a lefthanded batter, he had a definite advantage over right-handers. He seemed to be a miraculously created left-hander in both batting and hitting.

The Golden Rule of One Shot, One Kill

Lieutenant John introduced him to hunting and helped him practice the Golden Rule of "One shot = One kill," which meant that he should never fire any hunting bullet unless he is 100 percent confident that it will hit its target and kill the animal instantly to avoid any pain or suffering that are inflicted by injuring the hunted animal. He also taught him how to play and master baseball, utilizing his unique skill of the advantages of pitching with his left hand.

Over a period of four years, he participated in the New Hampshire hunting season (see figure 28). By using his left eye, he never missed any of his hunted targets and always practiced the principle of "One shot = One kill." He also won multiple Little League Baseball games. By being a left-hand pitcher, he was instrumental in helping his team win an important game in the New England Little League Baseball competition. The many baseball trophies and hunting awards decorated several of the orphanage's hallways.

Fig. 28. The New Hampshire hunting season

The Advantages of Left-handedness in Baseball

Since most players are right-handed, many are unfamiliar in dealing with those who are left-handed. Although only one in ten civilians are left- handed, one quarter of Major League Baseball players are southpaws. Left-handers get on base more frequently and pitch better than their righty counterparts. The left-handed batter is closer to first base, so he is getting a couple of steps advantage, trying to beat out a grounder. Also, as he swings, his momentum is turning him toward first base with another advantage that has to do with the angle of the ball. Three quarters of pitchers are right-handed. A righthanded batter has to look over his left shoulder, and the ball is coming at quite an angle. The offset of the eyes gives a depth perception, which is lost by looking over one's shoulder, leading to a considerable loss of distance between the two eyes, resulting in a tenth-of-a-second loss in seeing the ball, and that's why batters switch hit.

Mr. L had the advantage of already facing first base when at bat and easily kept an eye on first base when pitching and was able to visually cover a wide area of the outfield while wearing his glove on his right hand.

Other sports that offer an advantage to lefties are fencing, boxing, and tennis, which Mr. L considered to tackle at a future time if they come his way.

Carville—Marvels Revealed

Carville is a neighborhood of St. Gabriel in Iberville Parish in South Louisiana, located sixteen miles south of the capital city of Baton Rouge on the Mississippi River. It used to be the site of the United States Public Health Service National Leprosarium

Hospital, which for a hundred years treated patients with leprosy or Hansen's disease. The medical treatment facility closed its doors forever in 1999. The Carville's facilities were renovated and are currently operated by the Louisiana Army National Guard and include the National Hansen's Disease Museum, which has six thousand square feet of exhibits of patients' life, Hansen's disease and its cures, staff members, and the Daughters of Charity of St. Vincent de Paul, who played a vital role tending to and caring for patients with leprosy.

Dr. Paul Wilson Brand, who was born on July 17, 1914, and passed on July 8, 2003, grew up in India, studied medicine in London, and practiced orthopedic surgery in India and the US. He achieved world renown for his innovative techniques in the treatment of leprosy. He was a pioneer in developing tendon transfer techniques for use in the hands of those with leprosy. He was the first physician to appreciate that leprosy did not cause the rotting away of tissues but that it was the loss of the sensation of pain which made sufferers susceptible to injury. Dr. Brand contributed extensively to the fields of hand surgery and hand therapy through his publications and lectures. He wrote *Clinical Mechanics of the Hand*, still considered a classic in the field of hand surgery. He also wrote popular autobiographical books about his childhood, his parents' missionary work, and his philosophy about the valuable properties of pain. One of his best-known books, cowritten with Philip Yancey, was *Fearfully and Wonderfully Made*. This gold medallion award-winning book uncovers eternal statements that God has made in the very structure of our bodies, with captivating insights into the body of Christ. Before his death in 2003, Dr. Brand received many honors, including the prestigious Albert Lasker Award and appointment as Commander of the Order of the British Empire.

In a research project, I was invited along with other classmates, at the Tulane University School of Public Health and Tropical Medicine to spend a week at the National Hansen's Disease Hospital in Carville. I had the opportunity to interview one of the last cohorts of patients who were still residing at the hospital. Many patients who lost function in their limbs as a consequence of leprosy had reconstruction surgery. One of the patients, Mr. R, described with an immense sense of awe how his hand surgeon, who was trained by Dr. Brand, was able to reconstitute his left hand. Although he was born right-handed, he could not master playing the piano. He delineated the marvels of becoming left-handed as a consequence of the hand surgery. With his left hand, he was drawing breathtaking sunset sceneries of the ocean and playing piano concertos of Beethoven, Rachmaninov, Mozart, Brahms, and Tchaikovsky. Mr. R wanted to convey that despite the social stigma and his lifelong isolation at Carville, he would not trade any of his sufferings and his affliction with leprosy for any worldly material riches or rewards. His left hand was fearfully and wonderfully recreated by God's merciful love, Dr. Brand's instruction, and his hand surgeon skills. I contemplated for a while and, without revealing any personal information, took the risk of sharing Mr. R's narrative with Mr. L. In one brief sentence, he said, "Not all left hands are evil." I felt uplifted and looked forward to retrieving and reading Dr. Brand's book which was among my wife's most cherished library collections. I am in sincere gratitude to Dr. Brand, my wife Lynn, Mr. R, and Mr. L for the opportunity to read *Fearfully and Wonderfully Made* which became an invaluable source of reference in my career as a physician and a psychiatrist. I have retrieved it in so many clinical encounters with patients who were marveling at the miraculous creation of the human body.

CHAPTER 8

NEW HAMPSHIRE POLITICS— DESTINATION: VIETNAM

New Hampshire "Live Free or Die" and "First Presidential Primary State"

"Live Free or Die" is New Hampshire State motto found on all New Hampshire license plates, which ironically are inscribed on and prepared by prison inmates! The exact origin of the phrase, at least insofar as the New Hampshire motto is concerned, was' a famed revolutionary general from New Hampshire named John Stark, who was born in 1728.

Stark had a long and storied military career, but his lasting legacy is undoubtedly the New Hampshire motto. In 1809, when Stark was unable to attend a commemoration of the 1777 Battle of Bennington due to his old age and failing health, he sent along a letter to the gathered veterans instead. And at the end of that letter were the words that New Hampshire is now known for.

Throughout history, New Hampshire residents have fought hard to maintain their state as the first primary in the nation, claiming that it is their right to hold the first primary. Although across the country, many disagree with New Hampshire's right to host the first presidential primary. It is difficult to deny the pride and sense of responsibility the people of New Hampshire attach to the important role they play in nominating America's presidential candidates. That notion bears important facts about the historical importance of the state of New Hampshire in selecting USA presidents. New Hampshire voters are used to voting and are ranked among the highest in the presidential primaries; in addition, they are accustomed to voting since their governors have the shortest terms and have to be elected every two years.

Although Mr. L lived most of his childhood and teen years in New Hampshire, his life was totally insulated in the orphanage and he did not have the opportunities to experience the daily political life of the "Live Free or Die" state, except for the rare occasions he had with the Little League Baseball games, the various hunting events, and whenever he accompanied Lieutenant John to the political rallies during the presidential primary seasons (see figure 29).

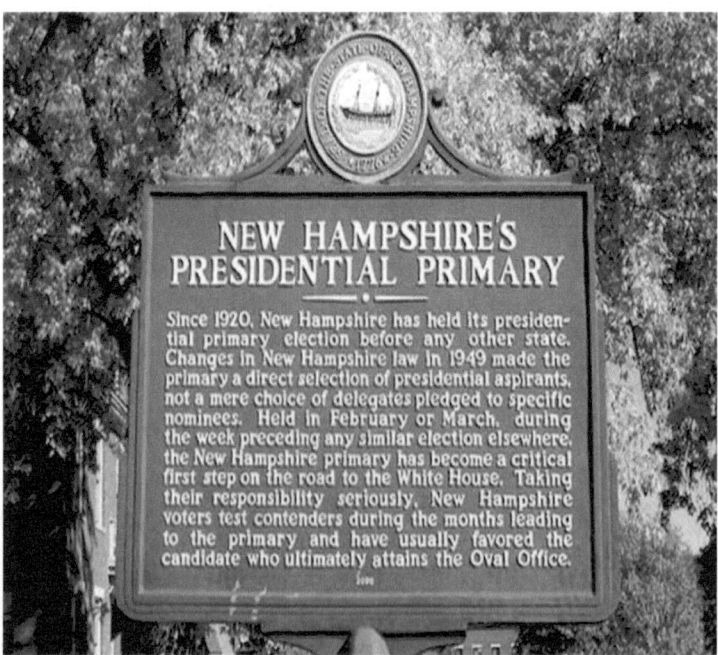

Fig. 29. New Hampshire Presidential Primary Declaration

The Vietnam War Military Draft Lottery

During the Vietnam War, young men gathered in college dorms and friends' homes to listen to live TV and radio broadcasts of the US Selective Service System, drawing lottery numbers to determine who would and would not be drafted. The military draft brought the Vietnam War to the American home front.

During that era, between 1964 and 1973, the US military drafted 2.2 million American men out of an eligible pool of twenty-seven million. Although only 25 percent of the military force in the combat zones were draftees, the system of conscription caused many young American men to volunteer for the armed forces in order to have more of a choice of which division in the military they would serve.

While many soldiers did support the war, at least initially, to others, the draft seemed like a death sentence for being sent to a war and fight for a cause that they did not believe in. Some sought refuge in college or parental deferments; others intentionally failed aptitude tests or otherwise evaded. Thousands also fled to Canada and the politically connected sought refuge in the National Guard, while a growing number engaged in direct resistance. Anti-war activists viewed the draft as immoral and a political mean for the government to continue the war with fresh soldiers.

Ironically, as the draft continued to fuel the war effort, it also intensified the anti-war cause. Although the Selective Service's deferment system meant that men of lower socioeconomic standing were most likely to be sent to the front lines, no one was completely safe from the draft. Almost every American was either eligible to go to war or knew someone who was.

Lyndon Johnson ran as the peace candidate in his 1964 campaign against conservative Barry Goldwater, who wanted to escalate the military offensive against North Vietnam and the Viet Cong guerillas. At a campaign appearance in Ohio, Johnson promised that "we are not about to send American boys 9 or 10,000 miles away from home to do what Asian boys ought to be doing for themselves." But in the months after the Gulf of tonkin Resolution, Johnson rapidly increased the US military presence in the defense of South Vietnam, with 184,000 troops stationed there by the end of 1965. During that pivotal year, the US military drafted 230,991 more young men. During the next four years, the Selective Service inducted an average of around 300,000 young men annually—including a significant percentage of the 58,156 American troops who would die in the conflict.

These contemporary important events were never seen or discussed by the peace-loving Carmelite nuns, and as a consequence, Mr. L was totally unaware of the military draft and was taken by a rude awakening surprise when, during a modest eighteenth birthday celebration, a man in a military uniform arrived to the orphanage and handed him his military draft lottery number (see figure 30)!

Fig. 30. The first Vietnam War draft lottery television broadcast

He was then drafted and ordered to report to his basic training station within a two-weeks period. He was confused. His brain felt foggy and dull, as if it was deeply penetrated by an invisible wound of despair and hopelessness. All the years of joy, love, and human attachment suddenly evaporated. He became numb and could only feel his early childhood emotion of anger, which escalated and reached its highest crescendo of absolute and unmatched inner void and detachment.

A Most Skilled Sniper with a Mission to Shoot to Kill

Mr. L was assigned to the United States Army, and later that year, he was declared as one of the best-skilled snipers in his division, with left-eye and left-hand advantages—although the word sniper evokes some unsettling imagery of a lone gunman that is undetectable and is on the hunt.

My son, Andrew, who has special interests in the military and is very knowledgeable of various types of military hardware and weaponry, educated and informed me that there is more to a sniper than just being an elite shooter who hide, line up a target in sight, and pull the trigger. When a sniper takes a shot, there are countless variables to consider before squeezing the trigger, such as wind speed, wind direction, range, target movement, mirage, light source, temperature, barometric pressure, and many other unpredictable variables.

Snipers are often perceived as lone assassins, racking up confirmed kills. In reality, committed and dedicated snipers are far more concerned with the number of lives they save than with the ones they take. Snipers are highly trained and specialize in shooting targets with modified rifles from incredibly long distances. They are also adept in stealth, camouflage, infiltration, and observation techniques. They are used in a variety of missions on the battlefield, and the sniper's primary mission has nothing to do with pulling a trigger.

When the mission calls for it, snipers can also dismantle and dishearten the enemy with a few well-placed rifle shots. Instead of engaging the entire enemy force like traditional infantry, snipers concentrate their efforts on hunting key people with deadly shots that kill without warning, and by doing so, snipers break both the enemy's will and its ability to fight. When there is no specific objective, a sniper will wait patiently for the unsuspecting targets to present the opportunity for a perfect shot.

On the day of his twentieth birthday, Mr. L was deployed to South Vietnam, where he was sent to Saigon, which was later renamed Ho Chi Minh City, and was stationed in a secret neighborhood that was monitoring all the traffic and movements around the USA Embassy. His sole objective was to target the would-be bicycle bomb detonators.

The Advantage of Being a Left-handed Sniper

Mr. L was praised by his commanders for being a left-handed sniper. He thought that he would endure a serious amount of prejudice. He knew that the word for left in almost every language has a less than positive connotation. With only about 10 percent of the population being left-handed, he had to survive and thrive since his earlier years in the orphanage's world, which was totally designed for those who are right-handed. Throughout his childhood and teen years, he experienced subtle advantages of being left-handed, such as it forced him to think more quickly, and for everyday life, he found it easier to multitask and deal with a large, sometimes unorganized stream of information.

As a left-handed sniper, he was assigned standard right-handed rifle in addition to a left-handed rifle. He was trained in using both types of rifles and was constantly reminded of his advantages over the right-handed sniper, because he could always keep his steady hand on the trigger without having to use it to cycle the bolt (see figure 31). This allowed him to keep looking through his scope, reload faster, and have a closer set up to the last shot that he took.

Fig. 31. A sniper's secret location near the American Embassy in Saigon

C H A P T E R 9
SAIGON AND ITS TURMOILS

The United States Embassy in Saigon

This embassy was first established on June 24, 1952, after the US Senate confirmed the first ambassador to South Vietnam, and was located at Thirty-nine *Hàm Nghi* Boulevard, and the original building remains there today. The embassy was the scene of a number of significant events of the Vietnam War, especially on March 30, 1965, with a Viet Cong attack, which occurred when a Vietnamese policeman began arguing with the driver of a car parked in front of the embassy but the driver refused to leave and then another Viet Cong member drove up alongside the car and fired on the policeman and the car, which contained 300 pounds of plastic explosives, detonated, and the five-story embassy building was in shambles. A new, bigger, and safer embassy was built in 1967 and was the scene of a number of significant events of the Vietnam War—most notably the Viet Cong attack during the tet Offensive, which helped turn American public opinion against the war, and the helicopter evacuation during the Fall of Saigon in 1975 (see figure 32). After which, the embassy closed permanently.

In 1995, the US and the Socialist Republic of Vietnam formally established relations, and the embassy grounds and building were handed back to the United States. The former embassy was s u b s e q u e n t l y demolished in 1998 and is currently a park inside the compound of the US Consulate General in Ho Chi Minh City.

Fig. 32. US Embassy evacuation from Saigon

Vietnam Bicycle Rider Bomb Detonators

The bicycle bomb detonator (see figure 33) is a bicycle rider who places an explosive device (or a bike bomb) on the bicycle and hide it so as to appear as an item that is being transported by the bicycle. Then when the intended target is reached, the bicycle rider detonates the bomb, leading to an explosion that blows up the rider and his target.

Fig. 33. South Vietnamese bicycle bomb detonation rider

103

Though Mr. L was the sniper assigned to shoot any suspicious bike rider nearing the USA embassy in Saigon, he worked and coordinated his mission with a spotter. His spotter carried his own special scope that is much more powerful than the scope on Mr. L's rifle. The spotter used his scope to help him in observing objectives and setting up the shot. Once the shot is taken, the spotter watched the shot to help him readjust his aim or his position in the unlikely event that he misses his target.

His relationship with his spotter grew in its strength and importance, and they depended on each other for survival and for executing their intended bike's detonators with the outmost and unmatched accuracy. He was surprised to realize that he was experiencing some degree of bonding with his spotter and nicknamed him Buddy. He remained guarded and hesitant in expressing any outward primary emotions toward Buddy and consolidated his emotional detachment.

An Orphanage in Saigon

During one of his time while off duty, Mr. L stumbled upon an orphanage in one of Saigon's neighborhood (see figure 34). Despite multiple warnings and arrests by the military police, he continued to visit that orphanage and brought all kinds of goodies to the orphans.

Fig. 34. Children residing in a Saigon orphanage

The nun in charge was Marie Nguyen, who happened to be fluent in French. One day, he received a letter from the Carmelite orphanage in New Hampshire, informing him that Soeur Marie was dying from cancer. His request to go to New Hampshire on an emergency military leave was denied by his commanders with a statement confirming that, as a sniper, he is "too valuable for the mission!" He later received a copy of her eulogy and a postcard, mentioning that she has left him a big wooden box. He was overwhelmed with fluctuating emotions of deep sadness to feelings of liberation, as if Soeur Marie's spirit was surrounding him and guiding him to get closer and closer to sister Marie Nguyen and the Vietnamese orphans.

About sixty-seven orphans (boys and girls), ranging in age from babies to preteens, shared bedrooms and slept primarily on mats, with a very limited outdoor space for activities. Sister Marie and three younger nuns, in addition to teaching the orphans reading and writing, prepared cooked meals for the older children and fed the babies with bottled milk. They also played table games, taught songs, and shared one-to-one time with each orphan. He instantly felt attached to all children and made a vow to devote all of his off-duty time to volunteer in that orphanage.

An Alleged Plot and Brutal Murders

Over a week course, Mr. L shot four suspected bicyclist bombers and was highly praised by his captain, who neglected to mention the valuable contributions of his spotter. From that moment on, his spotter, Buddy, along with other snipers, began to harbor deep resentment toward him. They planned a surprise twenty-third birthday event. They alleged that there was a credible evidence that three bicyclists will attempt to simultaneously detonate three bombs near a restaurant that is frequently crowded with American servicemen. He experienced an adrenaline rush[24] and did not follow proper procedures to verify that claim with his supervisor officers. He also forgot that he had promised Sister Marie Nguyen that he will help her build a barbed fence around the orphanage to prevent intruders and thieves who frequently trespassed in order to steal and vandalize.

The other snipers insisted that his skills are much needed to prevent the restaurant attack. He reluctantly agreed, and by midday, with his spotter coordination, he shot three bicycle riders. Later that evening, his spotter and the other snipers began singing, "Happy twenty-third birthday, happy three kills," then announced that it was all a hoax and that the three dead bicyclists were not bomb detonators.

He was overwhelmed with anger, guilt, and remorse. He aimed his riffle and stopped short of shooting his spotter and the other snipers. He felt as if his heart was exploding out of his chest and ran to the orphanage. The military police followed him. He reached the orphanage, and its entry door was busted. Sister Marie Nguyen and her three assistant nuns were brutally murdered. All the orphans were

---

24   Schmidt K. T., Weinshenker D., *Adrenaline Rush: The Role of Adrenergic Receptors in Stimulant-induced Behaviors, Mol Pharmacol* (2014), 85(4): 640–650.

kidnapped. A poster was hanging in the kitchen with big, red color letters that read in French, "*A small punishment for the left-eye and left-hand sniper. Wait for more to come.*"

He took a vow to revenge and started a fistfight with the military police, which led to a severe injury with profuse bleeding that required immediate on-the-field blood transfusion.

The Perils of an Adrenaline Rush!

Adrenaline, or epinephrine, is "a stress hormone secreted from the adrenal glands located on the kidneys." It plays a major role in preparing a person for an anticipated fight-or-flight reaction in threatening environments.

An *adrenaline rush* is "the sudden increase in the secretion of adrenaline from the adrenal glands, which happens when the brain communicates to the glands that there will be a need for a fight-or-flight response. An adrenaline rush could also occur during the absence of an actual physical threat but in response to an imagined threat, chronic stress, or severe anxiety. An adrenaline rush can have detrimental effects on physical and mental health and could affect the person's ability to rely on previously stored procedural memories in the context of making perfectly practiced and rehearsed critical decisions.

Mr. L was dismayed by the effects of his adrenaline rush on his judgment, and as a consequence, he rushed into targeting the three bicycle riders without reviewing the sniper's procedural manual—a book that he had memorized, in addition to neglecting the important and mandated requirement to obtain prior authorization from his supervisor officers. This tragic event gave birth to a deep sense of self-hatred with unbearable shame and guilt. He continued, however, to express his determination to kill his spotter and all the other snipers.

He refused to resume his military duties. He was flown out of Saigon with a new assignment to train United States Army snipers at the Stuttgart Base in Germany.

The Vietnam War—A Revered Connection

In 1987 following my completion of the psychiatry residency training, Dr. James Frank James (see figure 35) was the commissioner of mental health for the State of Oklahoma. As an attending faculty and a mentor, he kindly offered me an opportunity to join his staff in planning the inception of Oklahoma County Crisis Intervention Center (OCCIC). He had a vision to integrate the administrators of mental health services into the delivery of acute mental health services. All the administrators were relocated from their luxurious and well-furnished offices to the second floor of the OCCIC. Along with their clerical staff, they daily witnessed firsthand the complexity of providing timely and effective psychiatric emergency services.

Dr. James pioneered the concept of integrating therapeutic and supportive consultation with environmental modifications and intensive psychiatric interventions for those who are at risk of harming themselves or others and those with grave disability as a consequence of their psychiatric conditions. He devoted, in the midst of his extremely busy schedule, a weekly one-hour session to provide me with guidance and pearls of clinical insights to navigate the intricate components of compassionate psychiatric treatment within the frame of evidence-based practices. At times, I would lament the fact that if I was born in America, I would have been drafted and eventually sent to fight during the Vietnam War, which would have helped me grasp and understand the plights of the Vietnam War veterans. He would reflect and gently dismiss such a notion. I can still hear his kind words of reminding me of the universality of the human conditions regardless of your birthplace.

108

Over the course of four years of his dedication to teach and to train me as a third-year psychiatry resident and then an OCCIC staff psychiatrist, Dr. James never mentioned that he served at the rank of lieutenant commander in the US Navy as a flight surgeon during the Vietnam War (1963–1966), receiving the Combat Air Medal, Southeast Asia Expedition Medal, Vietnam Service Medal, Unit Commendation Medal. Additionally, Dr. James received the commanding officers' commendation for superior service aboard the USS *Kearsarge*, CV-33, rescuing downed pilots in North Vietnam. As a navy pilot, he flew twenty combat missions over North Vietnam. Dr. James Frank James passed away on November 26, 2018. He gave his life to the service of humanity with special dedication to alleviate the suffering of the mentally ill as he saved and changed countless lives. He will always be remembered for his joyful presence, his love for poetry, his masterful storytelling, his overflowing love and care for family and friends, and his kindness to all. My resentment to the untimely request of assessing Mr. L unexpectedly changed to moments of rejoice and revered remembrance of Dr. James as a mentor and a patriot. I was instantly transported to images of the Vietnam War's disheartening battles and silently wept.

Fig. 35. Dr. James Frank James

C H A P T E R 1 0

DECISION TO STARVE TO DEATH— DONE WITH THE MILITARY— WHAT'S AHEAD?

Torment in Germany

At the Stuttgart Base, Mr. L refused to obey orders and expressed daily feelings of despair and wishes to die because he could not bear the thoughts of what he did and what happened to the orphanage in Saigon. He did not believe in committing suicide, so he stopped eating and was placed in solitary confinement with forced feeding.

This type of extreme social isolation is usually aimed at making the confined person more amenable to persuasion, interrogation, or indoctrination to strictly abide by the rules and regulations of a military setting. Although isolation could probably be effective in the interrogation procedure, it can be easily counterproductive if not carefully monitored, in that confined person may react by telling their interrogators what they think they want to hear. The use of isolation to bring about ideological change and destruction of personal autonomy can be used to force a soldier to obey military commands and, in that particular case, was initiated to force Mr. L to perform his assigned military duty of training other snipers. It was maintained without excessive severity; however, he perceived it as a punitive measure, which magnified his wishes to be punished. So when he decided to combine it with firmly set determination to starve to death, his solitary confinement defeated its intended purpose. His commander found himself stuck and authorized the decision of forced feeding. As a consequence, solitary confinement did not accomplish its intended goal and became another tool for Mr.L to accomplish his own demise. He was on the brink of being court-martialed when urgent news arrived, announcing that, back in New Hampshire, Lieutenant John has died. This unexpected event, though tragic, gave the United State Army a rational to justify discharging Mr. L from the military service.

Discharged from the Military

A military discharge occurs when active military members are released from their obligation to continue service in the Armed Forces. A discharge relieves the soldier from any future military service obligations. There are several types of military discharges, including honorable discharge, general discharge under honorable conditions, other than honorable discharge, dishonorable discharge, entry-level separation, and bad conduct discharge that is usually issued by special court martial or general court martial. Despite his unmatched sniper and heroic performances during his services in Vietnam, he was not granted an honorable but rather a general discharge due to the events that led to his transfer to Germany. Mr. L felt that he deserved a dishonorable discharge based on his killing of the three innocent bicycle riders and continued to feel guilty and unworthy of living.

New Hampshire Estate and Inheritance Laws

The heirs of a deceased person in New Hampshire should immediately venture to their county's New Hampshire Probate

Court and begin the process of executing the estate. This procedure is most easily done with an estate worth $20,000 or less. A form called the petition for small estate administration will be filed by the heirs, and the process should be over in a matter of just a few months, with a court fee for filing.

With larger estates, the process becomes more difficult. Petitioners need to file other forms, such as the petition for estate administration, which names the person who will distribute the estate's funds. Fees just for this form and the cost of the entire procedure, including lawyer fees, might be around 10 percent of the estate's overall value. If there is a will, then one of the early goals of the New Hampshire Probate Court will be to validate the will. However, if there is none, then the probate process will be extended because of all the additional time that will be needed to decide which funds go to which heirs.

Mr. L was grieved and saddened and was hoping that Lieutenant John had a will that passed all his estate to his three daughters.

Unexpected Inheritance and Reminiscence

Mr. L returned to New Hampshire, wishing to die to only find out that Lieutenant John had a last will and testament, assigning him as the sole executer and inheritant of his estate, which included Lieutenant John's antique and gun shop. He wanted to give his inheritance to Lieutenant John's daughters—they refused. At his death bed, they promised their dad to abide by his last will and testament.

In New Hampshire, a will must be in writing with the testator, witnessed by at least two disinterested witnesses in the testator's presence, who attest to the testator's signature. Lieutenant John's will was declared as valid by the state and so was its clause, which prohibited giving his inheritance to the orphanage or to any charity. He wanted to die but did not believe in suicide.

He heard Soeur Marie's voice, "Mon chér petit garçon," as if she was somewhere around.

He gathered all of his inner strength to go visit the orphanage where he grew up, but it was no more in existence—only the chapel was left. He recalled, with endearment, Soeur Marie, telling him the history of the orphanage when its founder, a little nun, arrived in New Hampshire in 1913 and purchased it with an anonymous generous donor's contribution, and at that time, it only had two tiny frame houses. which became the heart of what has become the Carmelite orphanage. He remembered how the nuns' private rooms were adjacent to the children's living quarters for easy access and immediate availability.

Without his conscious awareness, his tears began to flow while reminiscing on the education that he received at this orphanage, which instilled within his whole being a distinct spirit that combined the contemplative and active living. He could repeat verbatim what he heard daily from the nuns: "We strive to live a life of daily servanthood that extend the love of Jesus to those around us."

His tears flew like a river downstream to his inner core. He could not grasp the reality of the orphanage's closure.

C H A P T E R 1 1

RELIEVING THE CHERISHED MEMORIES

The Heavy Wooden Box

Mr. L entered the chapel, hoping to instantly die by the altar. A custodian met him. He asked if there was anybody or anything left from the orphanage—nothing except a heavy wooden box (see figure 36) with a message in French, and it was addressed to Mon Chér Petit Garçon.

Fig. 36. The heavy wooden box

In that box were all the classic books, his essays, his baseball trophies, his hunting awards, and Soeur Marie's rosary with a special note, "Read, feel, and share your life's journey. I will be always nearby. You have been given to me as a heavenly gift."

Despite the high monitory value of his inheritance, he had a heavy feeling of not belonging and was deeply guilt-ridden for his shooting as a snipper using his left-hand and left-eye dominance and wished to be harshly punished and killed. So, to honor Lieutenant John's will, he chose to endure life. He converted the gun shop into a free-admission firearms museum and continued to acquire and to sell antiques. He built a modest one-bedroom apartment as a living dwelling and joined it to the antique shop and the firearms museum (see figure 37). He lived ten years of solitary life with a pervasive wish to never live another day. He realized and accepted the harsh reality that he could not change the past and that he has no control over his future. He found solace and peace in the wooden box of wonders that rekindled his acquired knowledge of the French language, the world literature, and the never-ending love of Soeur Marie. He refused to discard the older versions of himself and rediscovered the beauty of remembering the books he used to read, the people he used to care for, and all the hurts that he endured. He wished he could stop remembering because if he could just forget, maybe he would stop breathing. Soeur Marie's heavy wooden box was a constant reminder that his past would be an essential component in his building block of a future that is yet to come.

Fig. 37. Drawing of antique shop and house dwelling

Forgetting the Past

The past is impossible to forget. No matter how horrific or painful, it cannot be changed. Mr. L knew that what he chose to do with this memory of the past will certainly determine and shape his today. Since he wished to have no future and did not want to ever forget what he has done in the past, he wanted to use his memory of what happened in Vietnam as a constant reminder so he could be tormented every second of every minute of every hour of every day of his life as long as he is able to breathe.

However, this posed an unsurmountable dilemma. The past is also filled with the cherished memories of Soeur Marie and Lieutenant John. these memories always bring never-ending unconditional love and unmeasurable joy. He wished that these memories be erased so he could be only left with the agonizing memories of his time in Vietnam. If there was a laser beam or a gamma surgical knife that could pierce his skull and completely obliterate the cherished memories, he would use it and be left as long as he lives

116

with the painful memories to atone for his wrongful killing and to be punished for the Saigon orphanage's carnage.

He then, to his great astonishment, instantly recalled one of Soeur Marie's catechism class about who God is and found himself silently reciting the homework that he completed when he was thirteen years old!

Remembering the Catechism

Mr. L experienced a stream of memories about a catechism class describing several of God's attributes and character. He was reminded of who God is and that he is not just a "kind person or a magician," who responds on demand to his created humans' urgent, selfish, and self-centered needs but that he is the Almighty and Holy God, who does not trifle with evil, and that he is sovereign and is able to intervene in any situation if he is just asked that his will be done.

In the midst of his sufferings, he forgot that God has a plan and that God's wisdom is perfect. He needed to remember God's track record and that he has faithfully worked in his life prior to going to Vietnam. He also needed to remember how God has relentlessly worked through the lives of Soeur Marie and Lieutenant John, to show him his love. The God, who was faithful in the past, is always faithful in the present as well.

As he reflected on what grace meant to him when he lived in the orphanage, he recalled one of his favorite books, *Les Miserables* by Victor Hugo, where the released convict, Jean Valjean, who had been imprisoned for nineteen years for stealing a loaf of bread to feed his starving sister and her family, stopped at the home of a bishop and was shown great hospitality. But Valjean did not resist the great temptation before him. He stole some of the bishop's silver and ran off into the night. He was stopped by a constable and tried to lie his way out of trouble by saying that the silver was a gift. The constable took him back to the bishop, and Valjean expected the worst outcome of being sent back to prison. But the bishop, instead, surprised the constable by saying, "Of course this silver was my gift. But only part. You forgot the most valuable part. You forgot to take the silver candlesticks."

And before he departed, the bishop told Jean Valjean, "You must never forget this moment. Your soul and your life have been brought back. You are not your own. From now on, you belong to God."

He was granted grace, and for the rest of his life, he kept the candlesticks as a reminder of the grace that set him free.

Then Mr. L immediately recalled Soeur Marie words, "We would do well to find ways to remember God's grace."

That catechism lesson ended with the reminder about God's promises to his created humanity by memorizing them, displaying them, and reciting them as often as he can. He felt an inner peace about reflecting on the past in the context of remembering that God was still in the present as he was always in his past, as exemplified by Soeur Marie's mantra that God is always with us to forgive us, to provide for us, to see us through any circumstance, and to bring good, even from tragic times.

Despite these reassurances of God's character, faithfulness, grace, and promises, he was firmly convinced that these precious characteristics of God did not apply to his human condition and wished that he could be severely punished and killed.

O Fortuna

Mr. L mentioned that his wheel of fortune before he met Soeur Marie and following his return from Vietnam was and remained a fateful torment and, to my great surprise, elaborated on his intimate understanding of the German composer Carl Orff and his creative work Carmina Burana, which premiered on June 8, 1937, in Frankfurt. I heard it for the first time while listening to a radio broadcast debate about the human soul's temptation to succumb to the lure of indulging in pleasures. I did not understand its lyrics, which were written principally in Medieval Latin, Middle High German, and old Arpitan. The orchestration, chorus, and vocal soloists of this work of musical compositions left me with a longing and a yearning to watch it in a live performance.

In 1978, this dream became a reality when accompanied by the newlywed and dear friends Mona and Basem attended a *Carmina Burana* performance at the Royal Albert Hall in London. I vividly recall being transcended by the harmonious melodies in its prologue and epilogue, "O Fortuna" ("Oh Fortune"). This grandest statement in all choral literature depicts, with a stark warning, The power of luck and fate, framing the ancient image of a wheel of fortune that deals out triumph and disaster at random. Now and then, there are communities forced to wander and seek refuge from the caprices of cruel Fortune.triumph and tragedy continue their uneasy coexistence. I did not reveal my fondness for *Carmina Burana* and was overwhelmed with a prolonged paucity of verbal expression. Mr. L seemed to have detected my helplessness and eloquently suggested that I should listen to "O Fortuna" because it captures our tempest-tossed joys and struggles, and it suggests that for all our sakes, we try to steady Fortune's hand when her wheel seems about to spin out of control.

My silence unpredictably broke down, and without hesitation, I mentioned that Carl Orff 's brilliant Carmina Burana had and continues to enable numerous musicians, choruses, opera singers, and thousands of worldwide audience members to celebrate the triumphs—and bemoan the tribulations—of life and love. Mr. L then quoted scripture that he memorized in one of Soeur Marie's assignments: "*Do everything in love*" (1 Corinthians 16:14).

This statement offered a firm confirmation that my encounters with Mr. L were not just the consequences of mere coincidence that were ignited by an unwarranted psychiatric consultation but were indeed a series of predetermined providential events.

Surfing, Thinking, Writing, and Teaching

John Ernst Steinbeck Jr., an American author and a 1962 Nobel Prize laureate in literature, has been recognized for his realistic, imaginative writings; sympathetic humor; and keen social perception. Most of Steinbeck's works were set in central California, particularly in the Salinas Valley and the California Coast Ranges region in Monterey. He frequently explored the themes of fate and injustice, especially as applied to downtrodden or everyman protagonists. I was invited by a colleague, Dr. Neil Smith, to consider joining the Behavioral Health Department in Monterey County in Salinas where I was granted an incredible opportunity to work closely with Dr. David Penn Soskin (see figure 38), a compassionate and a gifted psychiatrist, who was devoted and committed to caring for the underserved—an exemplary portrayal of kindness and compassion not just for family, friends, and patients but even for perfect strangers. Dr. Soskin extended his generosity and welcoming attitude to make me feel at home in the clinical setting that is focused on addressing the needs of those afflicted with disabling and lifelong mental illnesses. On my daily drive from the Monterey coast to the heart of the Salinas Valley, I relieved with vivid imagery Steinbeck's The Red Pony, Of Mice and Men, Cannery Row, the multigeneration epic East of Eden, and the Pulitzer Prize—winning saga of the Grapes of Wrath. It was beautiful and heavenly to travel in Steinbeck's inspiring landscape and witness the hardworking farmers who continuously toil the land to grow the crops that sustain our lives. Dr. Soskin reintroduced me to the richness of Rumi's poetry, Tolstoy's novels, and the myth of Philoctetes as retold by Sophocles. He authored Open Source Psychiatry with essays about patient care, the use of technology to enhance medical care, and the potential of the internet to increase the viability and humanity of medical systems. The book also included his own poetry; hyperlinks to his educational videos, and materials for patients and clinicians, and his proof-of-concept protocols for testing novel antidepressants. Dr. Soskin received his bachelor and medical degrees from Harvard University and completed psychiatric residency at Harvard Medical School's Department of Psychiatry. He served on faculty at Harvard Medical School and as a principal investigator at the clinical research program. He created his own website as a resource for patients, clinicians, and researchers. He developed and copyrighted an algorithm to help readers find peer-reviewed and accessible scientific and medical articles. He left us on June 6, 2018, while recovering from a brain tumor surgery and courageously battling depression. His love for surfing, thinking, writing, and teaching surrounded me and guided me in recognizing, with a sad yet bright perspective, the many dimensions of Mr. L's enduring pains.

Fig. 38. Natividad Medical Center in Salinas

The Cairo Trilogy

Reflecting on the 1962 Nobel Prize laureate in literature, John Ernst Steinbeck Jr. evoked cherished remembrance of another Nobel Prize laureate in literature.The Egyptian novelist Naguib Mahfouz was awarded the 1988 Nobel Prize in Literature for The Cairo Trilogy. This trilogy narrates the rise and fall of the life of a tyrannical and ultraconservative father who lives in Cairo during World War I. He oppresses his wife, terrorizes his children, and leads a life of debauchery on the sly. Although he may be the ruler of the family, the person who enables it to function from day to day is his hardworking, slavishly docile, and incredibly submissive wife. His wife and children use different strategies to wriggle out from beneath his iron fist.The various members of this family weather the storms of Egyptian history during the first half of the twentieth century.They go through colonialist rule, revolutions, and two world wars. They find their own ways to cope with the political, cultural, and religious upheaval that surround their daily life.

The Cairo Trilogy was front and central to Naguib Mahfouz's insight and love for Egypt and its capital, Cairo, where he had weekly gatherings in various cafés. In these gatherings, friends, authors, novelists, artists, politicians, and students would meet to debate and discuss the sociopolitical and cultural issues of the day. In one of these cafés overlooking the Nile River, he was celebrated by friends and the general public when he was declared a Nobel Prize laureate in literature. My dear friend Samih invited me to attend some of the weekly gatherings at the Riche Café, where, as a novelist and a storyteller, Naguib Mahfouz offered the audience narrative streams of his novels' diverse variety of characters, which leave lasting impressions but also hold back something essential that is difficult to grasp. They turn up and disappear, leaving traces and clues but remaining enigmatic and ambiguous. They are figures in a greater story or pieces in a puzzle. Their lives are texts, continually being written and rewritten. Their appearance changes as the context alter with time and setting. Likewise, their meaning and purport depend upon viewpoint and perspective, and there are many layers of interpretation, from the gross to the subtle and inexpressible.

A correct hermeneutics or a right understanding is as evasive as the mirage of the nothingness of a vast expanse of desert. So do human illusions appear before us, materialize, and fade away, leaving voids pregnant with meaning. Naguib Mahfouz departed this life in August 2006 at the age of ninety-four, leaving behind much more than a legacy. He changed the way many people view the world, Egypt especially, and encouraged people to ask questions and challenge the status quo to understand why we are the way we are. He encouraged people to be honest and true, expressing his deeply held belief that this truth is what made the world so painfully beautiful. He has left his mark not only in Egypt but across the globe, capturing, forever and for everyone, an authentic and incredibly intimate portrayal of Egypt and her people.

Naguib Mahfouz reflected extensively on his core existence as Egypt's son, an identity that surpassed all of his innate gifts and talents as an author and a visionary. I was left to wonder about Mr. L's core identity. Is he just an orphan, an emotionally scarred sniper, a guilt- ridden soul? An inner voice affirmed to my wondering mind that he is unequivocally an authentic and genuine patriot and that I should constantly exert all efforts to elicit personal responses geared toward affirming that endeared aspect of his identity.

CHAPTER 12
THE BEGINNING—WWII

The Amazing Reunion

One day, a French-speaking middle-aged man appeared in the antique shop and announced that his name was Théodore and that he was Thérèse's son and that Lieutenant John was his father! He proceeded to tell the account of his father, John, meeting his mother, Thérèse, in France during WWII, with whom he fell in love instantly; however, her parents opposed their marriage. They pledged to each other to get married.

After his return to America, Lieutenant John lost contact with Thérèse. Ten years passed, and John married Marie, his high school sweetheart. twenty more years passed, and Thérèse found John's New Hampshire address, and she told him about their son, Théodore. She let John know that he is free from their pledge because she has been married to a distant cousin, and because they could not conceive, her husband adopted Théodore and raised him as his own and only child.

Théodore's story was confirmed by Lieutenant John's daughters, who had a photograph of their father sitting in a military vehicle that was driving through the French village where their dad met Thérèse (see figure 39).

Théodore knew about his father's last will and testament and refused Mr. L offer of surrendering all of his inheritance. He

Fig. 39. Photograph showing a military convoy driving through a French village during WWII

agreed to manage the museum and to maintain the adjacent house, to which Mr. L agreed without any hesitation.

Romantics and Europe Liberation

Between the years 1942 and 1952, about 1,000,000 American soldiers married women from fifty different countries. As many as 100,000 war brides were British—150,000 to 200,000 hailed from continental Europe, and another 16,000 came from Australia and New Zealand. There were brides from non-Allied countries too. Military estimates indicate that 50,000 to 100,000 servicemen wed women from countries of the Far East, including Japan, and immigration records show that by 1950, 14,175 German brides of American servicemen had entered the United States.

It's easy to imagine that young men experiencing lengthy deployments overseas would seek companionship. But what made so many foreign women enter relationships with American soldiers when their families and communities often disapproved of such unions? their decisions often came down to proximity, opportunity, and generosity. To the women of occupied France, American GIs were like a breath of fresh air. The soldiers' carefree, happy-go-lucky demeanor brought joy and light heartiness in the midst of the long years of gloomy darkness and hopelessness. The US military actively discouraged servicemen from marrying, believing family responsibilities would be a distraction. In fact, the military imposed many restrictions on marriages between servicemen and foreign women, mostly in vain. Back home, too, some American civilians decried the trend. There were those who defended the soldiers' right to marry whomever they wished, but others—especially single American women—were distressed at the idea of all those US troops bringing home foreign brides. The liberated people of continental Europe saw them as nothing short of heroes. Everywhere American troops went, as they swept through Europe in 1944, citizens rolled out the red carpet. Friendship with the Americans was not only accepted but also encouraged, although parents did have concerns about their daughters marrying the ingratiating foreigners.

Lieutenant John's relationship with Thérèse ended abruptly due to her parents' opposition and disagreement.

Oklahoma and the Trail of Tears

In 1830, Congress passed the Indian Removal Act, which required the various Indian tribes in today's southeastern US to give up their lands in exchange for federal territory, which was located west of the Mississippi River. The trail of tears was a series of forced displacements of approximately sixty thousand Native American Indians of the "five civilized tribes"—the Cherokee, Choctaws, Muscogee Creeks, Seminoles, and Chickasaws— to be relocated to the Indian territory which is present-day Oklahoma. The Cherokee removal in 1838 was the last forced removal east of the Mississippi, and it was brought on by the discovery of gold near Dahlonega, Georgia, in 1828, resulting in the Georgia Gold Rush. The impact on the Cherokee was devastating. Many of the old, the young, and the infirm died during their trip west, hundreds more deserted from the detachments, and an unknown number—perhaps several thousand—perished from the consequences of the forced migration.The tragic relocation was completed by the end of March 1839, and resettlement of tribal members in Oklahoma began soon afterward. The Cherokee, in the years that followed, struggled to reassert themselves in the new, unfamiliar land. Nowadays, they are a proud, independent tribe, and its members recognize that despite the adversity they have endured, they have developed a resilience with an unyielding commitment to invest in the perseverance of their ancestors'unique heritage and determination to pass it on to all of their future generations.

Native American: WWII in the South Pacific Theater

During the Psychiatry Residency training at the University of Oklahoma Health Sciences Center (OUHSC), my supervisor and attending psychiatrist, Dr. George H, Guthrey, recalled that after he graduated from medical school in 1944 at the age of 23, he joined the US Navy and was planning on becoming a surgeon. He was promised a fellowship in surgery at the Mayo Clinic upon his discharge from the Navy. During his WWII service, he spent six months taking care of Japanese prisoners of war in a South Pacific island. He then realized that most of the ailments of the Japanese prisoners such as headaches, stomach aches, and physical pain were related to emotional stress. This sparked his interest in psychiatry. So after the war and by 1948, Dr. Guthrey completed psychiatry residency at the Menninger Foundation in Topeka, Kansas. As a clinical professor of psychiatry at OUHSC and for forty-three years, he devoted his professional life to teach, educate, and train medical students, physicians in training, and psychiatry residents. His love of psychiatry and helping people permeated his life and was epitomized by a phrase etched in a building at the Menninger Foundation, "If only we can love." He once said about his work, "I love psychiatry. I get up every morning excited about the day ahead. I can't wait to see what's going to happen and something always does—no matter where I'm working."

Dr. Guthrey was a pioneer in mental health in Oklahoma and was highly respected by his peers. He was a lifelong volunteer in the mental health community and a Sunday school teacher. His favorite hobbies were golf and cooking, but his true skill lay in gin rummy and telling stories and jokes to his friends. His humor was a great asset. In addition, he was an accomplished violinist. He portrayed and practiced psychiatry as a unique dynamic medical specialty that is constantly moving on a quest to heal the human soul from the affliction of mental agonies. As a native Oklahoman, he knew firsthand and sympathized with the suffering of the Cherokee nation and the WWII veterans. In many of his mentoring sessions, he illustrated the healing power of faith, hope, and love. Although Dr. Guthrey departed from among our midst in 2005, his kindness and enduring legacy guided my response to Mr. L's statement when he adamantly rejected the notion of being healed and liberated from guilt if he could revive his faith, regain his hope, and rekindle his love. With a melodic voice he uttered, "How could it be? Was that doctor a disciple of Soeur Marie?"

I replied, "I am not sure, certainly Soeur Marie and Dr. Guthrey were a living example of the transforming powers of unconditional love."

He answered, "Doc, you are a dreamer, I am a realist. Some dreams are real, but most are just pure fantasies." He then whistled the melody of the song "Wind Beneath My Wings."

I wondered if he was reflecting on Soeur Marie and her role in lifting his spirit up from sadness and despair. I seemed to detect a sense of tranquility in these statements. I felt a sense of serenity and gratitude.

Destination Laos

He planned to board all of his home's windows with black wood. On his way to the store, he stopped to help a gentleman replace a blown car tire. The gentleman was wearing a hat with inscription from the Vietnam War. As they began to converse, he informed him that he belongs to a veterans' organization that was recruiting volunteers to remove land mines that were buried and left in fields in Laos since the Vietnam War. He felt an unexpected urge to join this organization, hoping that if he is accepted, he may be exposed to the opportunity of an accidental death while clearing some of these unexploded land mines. He applied to join that organization and, without any reservation, was accepted. He paid all of his travel and accommodation cost. He asked Théodore to try to sell his countryside home with the expectation that he will die and never return back to New Hampshire.

He arrived at the location in Laos that needed land mines clearance. He experienced a new sense of eagerness and enthusiasm, thinking that sooner than later, he will be totally and completely blown up by an unexploded mine and finally die. However, he was devastated when he saw the land mine victims, who were dismembered and in dire need of prosthetic legs and arms. He then realized that his constant preoccupation and the deep desires to step on a land mine evaporated and was instead occupied with Soeur Marie's and Sister Marie Nguyen's vivid images, surrounding him with their open arms, encouraging him to help these disabled victims. So with a cadre of local volunteers, he contributed his own money and built a prosthetic limbs workshop in a town near the land mines' infested region.

Over a period of three years, his workshop (see figure 40) provided prosthetic limbs to fifty-seven victims of unexploded Vietnam War land mines in Laos.

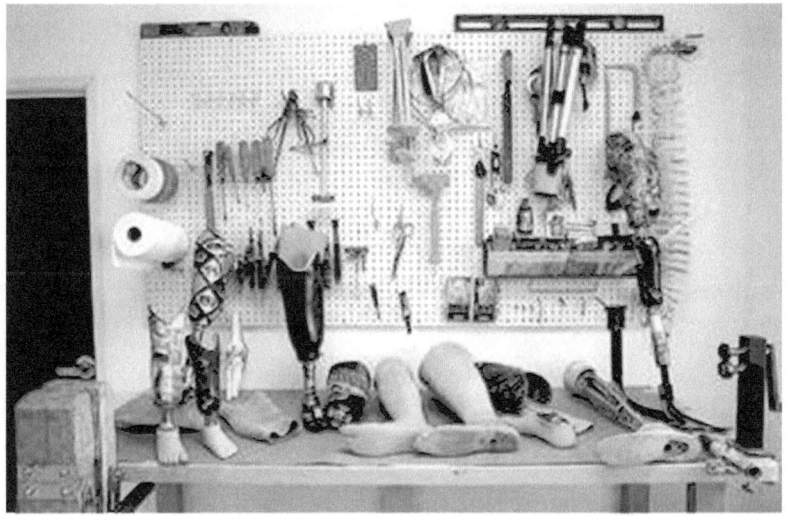

Fig. 40. Prosthetic limb workshop for land mine victims

Landmines—the Unseen Menaces of Human Lives

Mine is derived from the Latin word mina, which means "vein of ore" and was originally applied to the excavation of minerals from the earth. The term was then borrowed by military engineers, who excavate land mines during sieges.

During WWII, the Japanese military had a massive scale of land mines in a desperate move to delay and hamper the liberation of Philippines by advancing American troops.

It is estimated that 100,000,000 uncleared land mines lie

in the fields and alongside the roads and footpaths of one-third of the countries in the developing world. Claiming over 500 victims a week, land mines are weapons of mass destruction in slow motion. Around every twenty-two minutes, one person somewhere in the world is killed or injured by land mines. Unexploded land mines dot the periphery of the small country of Laos. The American legacy, stemming from the Vietnam War, has left the country with unexploded land mines, and between the years of 1999 and 2008, Landmine Monitor documented over 73,000 casualties. Just about 18,000 of these explosions resulted in death, with a staggering 32 percent children and 71 percent adults.

Laos averages about four new casualties a week from unexploded munitions. The Laotian government attributes a significant correlation between unexploded munitions and poverty.

Former US President Obama visited Laos in 2016, pledging 90,000,000 $ to clear unexploded ordnances, in addition to the $100,000,000 given over the last twenty years.

During his visit, President Obama stated that the US has a "moral obligation" to help the nation heal from the wounds of the war-riddled past. This historic event was the first time a sitting US president visited the country. He did not, however, offer an official apology.

War, fighting, and military actions are horrible, gross, and destructive events of civilians, their property and animals alike.

Princess Diana and Her Advocacy against Landmines

In January 1997, the Princess of Wales, Diana, called for an international ban on landmines.

At that time, she was visiting Angola and caught global attention by walking through a live minefield. Her trip is credited with boosting the campaign for a global landmine treaty signed later that year. At the time of Princess Diana's visit to Angola, Prince William and Prince Harry were fourteen and twelve years old, and her divorce from Prince Charles had been finalized the previous year. She was already known for her other charitable endeavors, such as her role in the 1987 opening of the UK's first HIV/AIDS unit in London, which was designed specifically to treat patients with the virus at a time when the illness was associated with social stigma and was not receiving appropriate comprehensive treatment. Princess Diana brought her signature determination to her campaigning against landmines. She had been involved with the British Red Cross for several years before the charity organized and supported her January 1997 trip to Angola. It was there in Huambo province that she came across the work of the Hazardous Area Life-support Organization (HALO) trust, which had been working to clear mines in Angola since 1994 amid the then-ongoing civil war, which ended in 2002 after more than twenty-five years of intermittent conflict. She met children who were landmine survivors, and she was also escorted by HALO students and mine-clearance experts through a cleared lane in one of the active minefields wearing protective armor and headgear (see figure 41). Images from her trip were immediately circulated across international media and provided a striking portrait of the princess among people in a humanitarian context. At the time of her visit in 1997, negotiations were ongoing to initiate the Mine Bans treaty. She had vocally appealed for an international ban on landmines during her time in Angola. Yet her efforts sparked criticism from the British lawmakers, who called her a "loose cannon" and out of line with government policy on the issue, which took a more cautious approach to negotiations about the use of landmines, which had not yet been banned in the UK. Despite the controversy, she had a significant impact on the political process that successfully banned landmines. Her tragic death in August that year created an added impetus for the treaty process. After her death, the Mine Bans treaty was drafted in Oslo, Norway, and took on the luster of a humanitarian memorial to Diana and her plight to ban landmines and their menaces.

Fig. 41. Princess Diana walking through a live minefield in Angola in 1997

Egypt, Struggles with WWII Land Mines

The arid desert of Alamein in northwestern Egypt continues to bear the traces of one of the most crucial battles of World War II, where the Second Battle of El Alamein took place, between October 23 and November 5, 1942, and tilted the balance of the conflict in North Africa in favor of the Allies. It is considered as important as the battles of Stalingrad and Midway, the other key clashes that marked the beginning of the defeat of the Axis powers.

Three cemeteries created amid Northeast Africa's desert sands honor the tens of thousands of soldiers from both sides who perished in the conflict. On a fateful date, after ongoing advances by German and Italian forces in the deserts of Libya and Egypt, the Allies managed to repel definitively their rivals' attempts to gain control of Egypt, marking a turning point in the balance of power of WWII.

In the field dedicated to the victors lies the remains of 7,970 British soldiers, in addition to others from Australia, New Zealand, India, and other countries that fought under the direction of Allied commander, Bernard Montgomery. The small, white cemeteries are built neatly on the sandy soil of the desert of Alamein, while each tomb has the name and nationality of the deceased soldier, except for unidentified combatants. The cemeteries are extremely well-kept, as a gardener comes every day to water the plants that decorate the enclosure, which houses a chapel and several monuments to honor nearly 12,000 soldiers, which were not recovered.

It was not easy to find and identify the remains of soldiers in the vast desert dotted by mines, while the defeated countries did so at the end of the war between 1949 and 1960, and afterward, they erected their corresponding funerary monuments. On the shores of the Mediterranean Sea, a tall and imposing octagonal tower of white stone emerges, where the remains of 4,634 Italians, about half of them are unidentified, lie (see figure 42). For Germans, medieval-style cemeteries were created with the remains of 4,313 soldiers of the Third Reich (see figure 43).

Fig. 42. Italian WWII Memorial in El-Alamein, Egypt

Fig. 43. WW-II German Memorial in El-Alamein, Egypt

The Battle of El-Alamein is heralded as a crucial victory for the Allies that decisively turned the tide on Italian and German forces in North Africa. But for locals on the ground, the event that British leader Winston Churchill famously called the "end of the beginning" of the war has left a threat that remains three quarters of a century later.

El-Alamein may have stopped 75 years ago, but Egypt is still waging another war against the hidden enemy of land mines by a painstaking work of mining explosives and detonators across the vast stretch of sand as they showcased the deadly legacy left behind by the Axis and Allied troops, who wrestled for control along the Mediterranean coast.

Although some 1,000 square kilometers have cleared of these land mines, huge swathes of territory of approximately 2,680 square kilometers of the land in the Northwest Coast are estimated to still be contaminated. The presence of land mines in and around El-Alamein has not just exacted a heavy toll on residents—it has also stunted economic development in a seaside region that could be a tourist draw. Explosives constitute a huge obstacle to the socioeconomic development of the region, which is known for its rich natural resources.

Part of an ambitious government program to create more than thirty cities from scratch around the country to alleviate Egypt's urban crush, new Alamein is being built on an area that has been cleared of explosives. It is hoped that the city will provide a vital economic boost for the country, providing almost 300,000 jobs and attracting people from densely populated areas. This project would be paving the way for the establishment of the new city of El-Alamein with promising future economic opportunities.

El-Alamein, Moon Landing, and a Tribute to a Beloved Friend

On May 25, 1961, President John F. Kennedy announced, before a special joint session of congress, the dramatic and ambitious goal of sending an American safely to the moon before the end of the decade. The decision involved much consideration before making it public, as well as enormous human efforts and expenditures to make what became Project Apollo a reality. Only the construction of the Panama Canal in modern peacetime and the Manhattan Project in wartime were comparable in scope. President Kennedy was assassinated in 1963, and although he did not witness the completion of this unprecedented exploration, his wish came true in less than ten years. On July 20, 1969, Apollo 11 commander Neil Armstrong and astronaut Edwin "Buzz" Aldrin stepped off the Lunar Module and landed on the moon's surface.

In addition to the US flag, they also left a sign on the moon, which read: "Here men from the planet Earth first set foot upon the moon. July 1969 AD. We came in peace for all mankind."

Pére Maurice Martin a French Jesuit priest who, during his seminary years, felt the call to serve in Egypt. His supervisors insisted that he would not be sent to Egypt until he mastered the Arabic language with its distinct Egyptian dialect—a task that is extremely difficult for most linguistics and especially for francophones. He accepted and fulfilled this insurmountable requirement and was eventually sent to the Jesuit's school in Cairo, Egypt. He became one of my spiritual mentors and teachers during my secondary-school years. He challenged me along with my lifelong friend Adel Sabet to step out of our circle of close friends and cozy life. He asked if we could practice the tenants of the Jesuits' education and reach out to encourage and inspire a younger generation of secondary-school students who were attending a regular public school. He introduced us to the concept of the servant leader[25]—an approach that puts serving others above all other priorities by focusing on creating an environment in which team members thrive and successfully achieve their set goals. It is a selfless leadership style that aspires on promoting the long-term growth of team members. Over a course of two years, we spent many weekends and holidays in the Cairo neighborhood of Sharabeya—an area that had primary and secondary schools in the midst of overcrowded homes. With Pére Maurice Martin's relentless support, he encouraged us to befriend several students of that neighborhood and to name just a few: Karem Kirollos, Talaat Tadros, Mounir Iskander, and Adel Halim. We initiated a group modeled after the boy scouts' motto that was devised in 1907 by the English soldier Baden-Powell. The motto simply emphasized the basic fundamentals of being always "ready and prepared" in mind and body to complete any assigned duty. In addition to participating in service projects in Sharabeya. The team set a plan to test endurance and commitment to a specific and challenging task. A goal was set to walk 162 miles from Cairo to the desert of El-Alamein and reach this destination on July 20, 1969—the same day when the world was captivated by the first landing of a man on the moon. This proposed adventure took months of preparation and was ultimately accomplished by walking during the day and camping at night along Egypt's mediterranean coast. Throughout the twenty-one-day journey. every team member practiced serving and attending to the daily needs of other members and bystanders encountered along the traveling routes. Avoidance of the perils and dangers of El-Alamein's unearthed land mines was a constant daily exercise of mental alertness and vigilance. In an impromptu visit to St. Mina (Menas) Coptic Orthodox Monastery in Mariut, near Alexandria,

---

25   Gagarin, M. (ed.), "Christian Art in Egypt" in the *Oxford Encyclopedia of Ancient Greece and Rome* (Oxford/New York: 2010), vol. 2, pp. 101–103.

some of the monks residing at the monastery expressed concerns about the danger of walking on shifting desert sand. At the time, Pope Kyrillos of the Coptic Orthodox Church was staying at the monastery for a period of fasting and spiritual retreat. Despite his seemingly surprised eyes expression, Pope Kyrillos bestowed upon our group his blessings and prayers of protection while traveling. He commended five dogs to guide us through many detours in the wide-open desert, and we safely arrived at our beach camped tents. In the tenth year of his papacy, Pope Kyrillos was known for his humility and piety. His name Kyrillos in Arabic meant "the man of prayer." During his Papacy, he celebrated the inauguration of the new St. Mark Cathedral in Cairo. This celebration coincided with the return of the relics of St. Mark the Apostle from Rome after being in the city of Venice in Italy for eleven centuries. We remain forever grateful for Pope Kyrillos's prayers and the protection he granted our group which certainly spared us from the unknown perils of a shifting desert sand.

Egypt's Coptic Church

The word *Copt* is derived from the Greek word *Aigyptos* (Αἴγυπτος), which was, in turn, derived from "Hikaptah," one of the names for Memphis, the first capital of Ancient Egypt. The modern use of the term *Coptic* describes Egyptian Christians, as well as the last stage of the ancient Egyptian language script. It also describes the distinctive art and architecture that developed as an early expression of the Christian faith. The Coptic Church is based on the teachings of St. Mark who wrote the second of the four gospels and who brought Christianity to Egypt during the reign of the Roman Emperor Nero in the first century. Although fully integrated into the body of modern Egyptian society, the Coptic Church regards itself as a strong defendant of the Christian faith. The Nicene Creed, which is recited in all churches throughout the world, has been authored by one of its favorite sons, St. Athanasius— the Pope of Alexandria for forty-six years, from 327 AD to 373 AD. The contributions of the Coptic Church to Christendom are many. From the beginning, it played a central role in Christian theology and, specially, to protect it from the Gnostics heresies. The Coptic Church produced thousands of texts, biblical and theological studies which are considered important archeological resources. The Holy Bible was translated to the Coptic language in the second century. Despite centuries of persecution, the Coptic Church as a religious institution has never been controlled or allowed itself to control the governments in Egypt. This long-held position of the church concerning the separation between state and religion stems from the words of the Lord Jesus Christ himself when he asked his followers to submit to their rulers: "Render therefore to Caesar the things that are Caesar's, and to God the things that are God's" (Matthew 22:21). The Coptic Church has never forcefully resisted authorities or invaders and was never allied with any powers, for the words of the Lord Jesus Christ are clear: "Put your sword in its place, for all who take the sword will perish by the sword" (Matthew 26:52). The miraculous survival of the Coptic Church till this day and age is a living proof   of the validity and wisdom of these teachings. The Coptic Orthodox Church's clergy is headed by the Pope of Alexandria and includes bishops who oversee the priests ordained in their dioceses. Both the Pope and the bishops must be monks; they are all members of the Coptic Orthodox Holy Synod (council), which meets regularly to oversee matters of faith and pastorship in the church. The Cardinal of the Coptic Catholic Church sui juris comprises a single ecclesiastical province, covering and retaining the ancient title Alexandria, but his actual seat is in Egypt's capital, Cairo.

Daily, in all Coptic Orthodox and Catholic Churches all over the world, they pray for the reunion of all Christian churches. They pray for Egypt, its Nile, its crops, its president, its army, its government, and, above all, its people. They pray for the world's peace and for the well- being of the whole human race.

Mr. L's dedication to the land mines clearance in Laos ignited and triggered vivid relieving of Pope Kyrillos and Pére Maurice Martin's kind teaching about the abundant fruits that thrive and grow in the inner being of a servant leader. My heart began pounding with gratitude toward my beloved friend Adel Sabet, who unexpectedly was taken away from our midst. He was a devoted husband, father, grandfather, and teacher who, for five decades, taught his secondary-school students the values of adhering to moral convictions in the face of adversity and the lures of materialism. What would have happened if I had rejected the notion of interviewing Mr. L? I would have certainly missed a unique and probably once-in-a-lifetime golden opportunity of reminiscing the Sharabeya group, the El-Alamein adventure, the landing on the moon, and the legacy of Adel Sabet's precious life of selfless giving—a stewardess of the poor, the helpless, and the disfranchised. Students who shared in serving projects in Sharabeya included among others Raouf Amin, Nagy Tawfic, May Acoury, Richard Hamamdjian, Rafik Sidawi, Gilbert Hamamdjian, Ezzat Kozman, Amal Assa'ad and Nahla Acoury. Navigating the call of serving the Sharabeya group while fulfilling the rigors of medical school attendance was challenging and, at times, difficult. During these challenging times, I was surrounded by the flowing support of my family and my medical school friends and colleagues, Nabil Badra and Kamel Schoucralla.

CHAPTER13

DEATH, THE ULTIMATE PUNISHMENT

A Roof Collapses and a Hand Injury

A thunderstorm with lightning ignited a fire, and the prosthetic limbs workshop and its roof collapsed. Mr. L's left hand was severely injured but not burned. He was evacuated and transferred to the Veteran Affairs (VA) hospital in Manila, then later flown to the Washington, D.C., VA Hospital and on New Year's Eve, a successful surgery led to the complete restoration of his left-hand middle finger. This was a disappointing result since he wished to have lost this left evil hand, especially with its trigger finger that killed the innocents. He was informed that he has the hepatitis C virus infection, which was attributed to the blood transfusion he had received during his service in Vietnam. He rejoiced when he heard this news because he saw it as a deserved punishment. He wanted the prosthetic limbs workshop to be rebuilt in a way that could prevent future damages related to increment weather conditions. So, he liquidated all of his remaining financial assets, including the money he earned when Théodore sold his home in New Hampshire and donated it all to the local town health authorities in Laos.

As a transgressor who killed the innocents and led to the massacre of the helpless, he was looking and searching for means of restitution. He could not restore the cyclists', the orphans', and the nuns' lives. In his case, restitution and repentance were impossible. He could not bring back to life those who have been killed because

143

of his actions. Thus, in order for justice to be executed, he finally found the ultimate punishment. By refusing hepatitis C treatment, he will surely die and pay the price for his crimes.

Perfect Timing for a Final Judgment and Punishment

He seemed to cherish the fact of being infected with the hepatitis C virus. He realized that he was now financially broken, homeless, and infected with a possibly deadly virus. He assumed that if he was not treated, the infection would surely lead to his final demise and, ultimately, death, and in a way, that would be his final judgment and punishment for killing the innocents with his *evil* left hand using his *evil* left eye.

Prior to his hospital discharge, a psychiatric consultation was called to recommend treatment for depression. A medical student and a psychiatry resident evaluated him and diagnosed him with two psychiatric conditions: reactive attachment disorder (see figure 12) and posttraumatic stress disorder (see figure 13). The psychiatric attending also confirmed both conditions[26] and recommended prompt psychiatric interventions. He rejected the psychiatric recommendations, refused any medical intervention for hepatitis C, and insisted on leaving the hospital, so he was discharged against medical advice.

Deep inside, he felt scared and was longing to hear Soeur Marie's reassuring voice to only experience a total and serene silence. He excelled with a sigh of relief and heard his inner voice: "Your punishment has been executed, and at last you are free to die."

---

26   American Psychiatric Association, *Diagnostic and Statistical Manual of Mental Disorders, 5th edition* (Arlington, Virginia: 2013), 265–268 and 271–280.

The Vietnam War Moving Wall Memorial

James was another Vietnam War veteran, who was recovering from a shoulder surgery and was in a nearby recovery bed. He was infuriated at Mr.L's attitude and insulted him, described him as a coward. How can he refuse to live while many thousands of soldiers died in Vietnam, leaving their loved ones behind, wishing that they were in his place?

He then asked him if he knew about the Vietnam War Moving Wall Memorial (see figure 44). Without waiting for answer, he proceeded to tell him that it is a half-size replica of the Vietnam War Memorial in Washington, D.C. (see figure 45). It was first displayed in Tyler, Texas, in October of 1984. It was devised to give Vietnam War veterans, their friends and families, who could not travel to Washington, D.C., the opportunity to see The Wall in their own home state.

Fig. 44. A display of the Vietnam War Moving Wall Memorial

Fig. 45. Vietnam War Wall Memorial in Washington, D.C.

Two structures of the moving wall travelled the United States from April through November, spending five or six days at each site (see figure 46). On its visits, the moving wall is often escorted by state troopers or volunteer organizations and Vietnam War veterans, who accompany the memorial on motorcycles.

Fig. 46. Transporting the Vietnam War Moving Wall
Memorial

James assertively asked him to join the volunteers who escort the moving wall (see figure 47) and to also accept the offer to be treated for his viral hepatitis C infection!

Fig. 47. Escort of the Vietnam War Moving Wall Memorial

He adamantly refused James suggestions and asked him to forget that they have ever met. However, James contacted the Veterans of Foreign Wars Organization and provided them with Mr.L and his circumstances.

The Vietnam War Wall Memorial History

The Vietnam Veterans Memorial, also called The Wall, is one of the national monuments in Washington, D.C., that was designed to honor members of the US Armed Forces, who served and died in the Vietnam War (1955–1975).

The memorial is located near the western end of the Washington, D.C., mall. It is a black, granite, V-shaped wall inscribed with the names of the approximately 58,000 men and women who died or were missing in action during the Vietnam War (see figure 45). It was designed by the American architect Maya Lin.

When Maya was twenty-one years old and an undergraduate student at Yale University, she entered a nationwide competition sponsored by the Vietnam Veterans Memorial Fund, and her design was selected from the more than 1,400 submissions that were received. Lin's minimal plan was in sharp contrast to the traditional format for a memorial, which usually included figurative heroic sculpture. The design aroused a great deal of controversy, reflecting the lack of resolution of the national conflicts over the war, as well as the lack of consensus over what constituted an appropriate memorial at the end of the twentieth century.

Eventually, a compromise was reached with the commissioning of a traditional statue, depicting three servicemen with a flag, to stand at the entrance to the memorial. After Lin's monument was dedicated on November 13, 1982, it became a popular and an emotionally moving tourist attraction. On November 11, 1984, the servicemen statue and a US flag were formally added to the memorial, and the combined monument was placed under the control of the National Park Service.

In 1993, the Vietnam Women's Memorial was unveiled a short distance from The Wall. The bronze sculpture, depicting three women caring for an injured soldier, recognized the work of the more than 10,000 women who served in Vietnam.

In 2009, the Vietnam Veterans Memorial Fund assumed responsibility for the maintenance of the site.

Veterans of Foreign Wars

The Veterans of Foreign Wars (VFW), also known as the Veterans of Foreign Wars of the United States, Inc., is an American veterans' organization established on September 29, 1899, by soldiers, sailors, marines, and airmen, who served the US in wars, campaigns, and expeditions on foreign soil or hostile water.[27]

The purpose of the VFW is to speed rehabilitation of the nation's disabled and needy veterans, assist veterans' widows and orphans and the dependents of needy or disabled veterans, and promote Americanism by means of education in patriotism and by constructive service to local communities.

The organization maintains both its legislative service and central office of its national rehabilitation service in Washington, D.C. The latter nationwide program serves disabled veterans of all wars, members and nonmembers alike, in matters of US government compensation and pension claims, hospitalization, civil service employment preference, and any other needed services.[28]

The VFW offers a wide range of assistance programs that include providing free, professional help filing or appealing a VA claim, offering scholarships for postsecondary education, or providing emergency financial relief when times get tough. The VFW National Veterans Service program consists of a nationwide network of VA accredited service officers and predischarge representatives, who are highly trained, and professional experts that also act as advocates to help veterans cut through bureaucratic red tape.

---

27   Veterans of Foreign Wars (VFW), Encyclopædia Britannica (2015), retrieved November 14, 2016.

28   Ibid.

Mr.L did not want to seek or to be contacted by the VFW.

Rescue in the Midst of Despair

The VFW intently attempted to find Mr. L to no avail since he did not have any known address. In the meantime, he was hoping to resume his quest to die by starving himself while residing in a homeless shelter in New Hampshire.

One day, while sitting under a frozen bridge, a person stopped and, assuming that he was a beggar, handed him a $20 bill. He looked up, and that person was Théodore, Lieutenant John's son, who burst into uncontrolled tears and kept weeping while hugging him. Despite his emotional resistance and feelings of detachment, Théodore insisted on calling all of Lieutenant John's daughters, and Priscilla, the youngest daughter, rushed to the scene and was accompanied by her husband who was an Army officer and, without his knowledge, contacted the New Hampshire's chapter of VFW.

A chain of unpredictable events occurred all at once and ended with Théodore reaching James, who issued a verbal ultimatum through his mobile phone in which he warned him that if he did not follow the VFWs instructions, he will contact the sheriff 's department and would inform the officers about his plan of starving himself to death, which would be a ground to an involuntary psychiatric hospitalization.

CHAPTER14

LOOMING CRISIS AND FINANCIAL COMPENSATION

Involuntary Emergency Admission (IEA)

The IEA process begins with a visit to a local hospital's emergency department or a community mental health center and the completion of an IEA petition, requesting admission to New Hampshire Hospital. The person being admitted must pose a likelihood of danger to self or others as a result of a mental health condition. The person who signs the petition is the petitioner. Other witnesses to the person's behavior may also describe those behaviors on the petition.

Financial Compensation

Because he contracted hepatitis C during his service in Vietnam and because of the traumatic events he witnessed and experienced during his service with the Army, the VFW became involved, and his discharge from military service was changed from regular to honorable.

Mr. L was awarded a service connection disability with financial compensation for posttraumatic stress disorder (PTSD) with thousands of dollars of back pay compensation. He also qualified for treatment of hepatitis C. Unexpectedly, he heard Soeur Marie's loving voice, urging him to accept his newfound friend James's suggestion and to express gratitude to Théodore, Priscilla, and her husband, which he did without any hesitation.

He received treatment for hepatitis C, and to the total surprise and utter amazement of his treating doctors, although not cured, his blood had a very low count of the hepatitis C virus.

Service Connection Disability

Disability compensation is a monetary benefit paid to veterans who are determined to be disabled by an injury or illness that was incurred or aggravated during active military service. These disabilities are considered to be service connected. To be eligible for compensation, the veteran must have been separated or discharged under conditions other than dishonorable. Monthly disability compensation varies with the degree of disability and the number of eligible dependents, and in his case, he was granted 100 percent service connection disability for chronic and severe PTSD.

Veterans with certain severe disabilities may be eligible for additional special monthly compensation. The effective date for disability compensation benefits is usually the date of receiving the application. Disability benefits will be due from the first day of the month, following the month of the effective date. Because it takes months or years to decide applications, veterans can expect back payments going back many months once they are approved. Disability compensation benefits are not subject to federal or state income tax. In addition to his monthly disability income of $2,858.24, Mr. L also received a lump sum back payment of $20,150.00.

Without James insistence, he would have given away all of this disability income.

State of the Art Treatment of Hepatitis C Infection

Many veterans contracted hepatitis C infection during their service in the Vietnam War as a result of battlefield injuries requiring blood transfusions, later suffering from the consequences of this largely silent menace, which causes liver inflammation or hepatitis, cirrhosis, and liver cancer. Without treatment, some would certainly die.

The VA has assumed a leadership role in hepatitis C screening, testing, treatment, research, and prevention. Over the past few years, tens of thousands of veterans enrolled in VA care have been successfully treated for hepatitis C. New treatments are able to cure most people of hepatitis C after about twelve weeks of treatment.

VA expects that with ongoing expansion of hepatitis C treatment, many more veterans will be started on hepatitis C treatment every week. In addition to furnishing clinical care to veterans with hepatitis C, VA research continues to expand the knowledge base regarding the disease through scientific studies focused on effective care, screening, and health care delivery to include veterans with complicated medical conditions in addition to hepatitis C.

Mr. L benefited from hepatitis C treatment and did not exhibit any residual symptoms of that infection.

Motorcycle Rides

James urged Mr. L to use his money wisely, and he was encouraged by other Vietnam War veterans, whom he met while receiving the hepatitis C treatment, to join the motorcycle club—to ride in procession of the Vietnam War Moving Wall Memorial when it travels between various towns and cities (see figure 47).

153

The wish to die was still forefront on his mind and non-abatable, and he wanted to reject the notion that he has PTSD so he can return the money that he was awarded for that condition. He set out a goal to achieve, and that was to disprove that he has PTSD.

CHAPTER 15

SCIENTIFIC APPROACH TO BRAIN FUNCTIONING

The 1990—the Decade of the Brain

President George H. W. Bush proclaimed the decade beginning January 1, 1990, as the Decade of the Brain. He called upon all public officials and the people of the United States to observe that decade with appropriate programs, ceremonies, and activities. During the period of the Decade of the Brain, the field of neuroscience made rapid gains and, in several important ways, rose to the forefront of both scientific and public interest. It engaged scientists, legislators, and leaders of voluntary agencies.

Several scientific accomplishments occurred during the Decade of the Brain, which included the development of functional magnetic resonance imaging (fMRI), neural imaging, and the emergence of the field of computational neuroscience, leading to the discovery of neural plasticity and critical periods of neural development; the development of second-generation antidepressant and antipsychotic medications; the discovery of genetic mutations responsible for Huntington's disease, Amyotrophic lateral sclerosis (ALS) or Lou Gehrig's disease and Rett syndrome.

Society also benefited from the Decade through major cash infusions into early childhood development programs. Due to the funding of research into the physiological impact on the brain of children's early experiences, many states in the US began to implement new programs for preschool education. The Decade of the Brain also inspired the conception of the Decade of the Mind.

Biological Correlates of PTSD

Through his extensive reading about brain imaging, Mr. L acquired knowledge and understanding about the various brain structures and had a keen interest in the limbic system[29] and particularly the amygdala and the hippocampus (see figure 48).

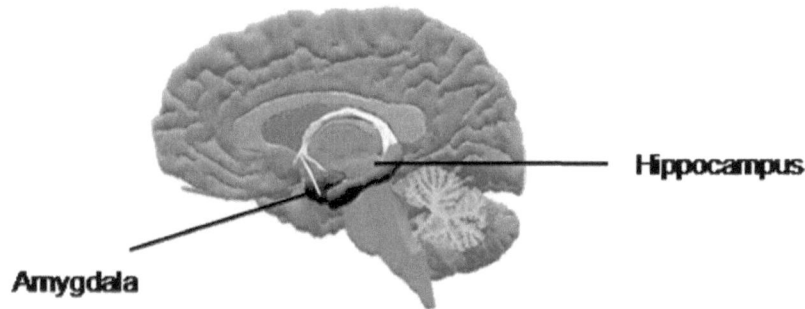

Fig. 48. The amygdala and the hippocampus

The limbic system structures are involved in many emotions and motivations related to survival, such as fear, anger, reward, and pleasure, such as those experienced from eating and sexual activities. the limbic system influences both the peripheral nervous system and the endocrine system.

The amygdala is responsible for determining which memories are stored and where the memories are stored in the brain. It is thought that this determination is based on how large an emotional response an event invokes. The hippocampus sends memories out

---

29   Jorge R. E., "Posttraumatic Stress Disorder," in *Behavioral Neurology and Neuropsychiatry, no. 3* (Continuum: Minneapolis, Minnesota. June 21, 2015), pp. 789–805.

to the appropriate part of the cerebral hemisphere for long-term storage and retrieves them when necessary. Damage to this area of the brain may result in an inability to form new memories.

The hippocampus is a brain structure that is named due to its resemblance to the seahorse, from the Greek ἱππόκαμπος, *seahorse* from ἵππος hippos, *horse* and κάμπος *kampos*, "sea monster."The hippocampus is located under the cerebral cortex (see figure 49).

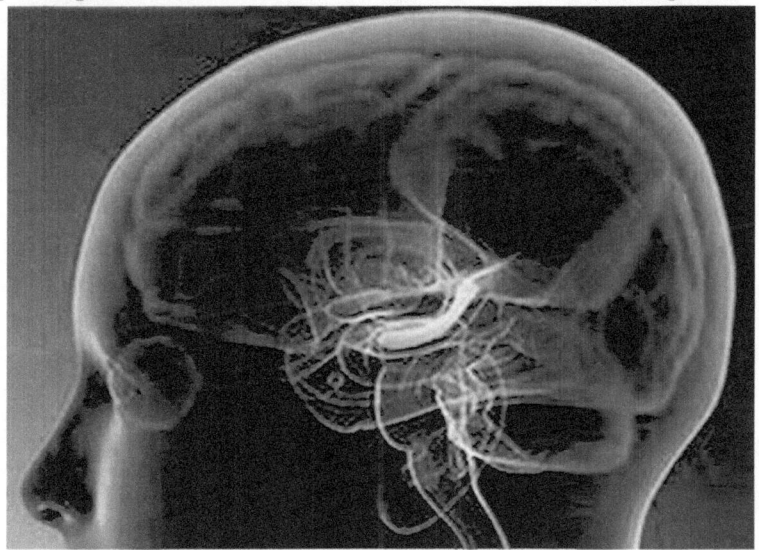

Fig. 49. Location of the hippocampus

Mr. L recognized the values of the implementation of the Decade of the Brain initiatives, so he decided to enroll in one of the Clinical Neuroscience Research Division at the VA in New Hampshire, hoping to disprove his PTSD diagnosis. His MRI and positron-emission tomography (PET) scans showed bilateral normal amygdala size and increased hippocampus size (see figure 50), which did not match the decreased sizes of these structures in many individuals with PTSD.

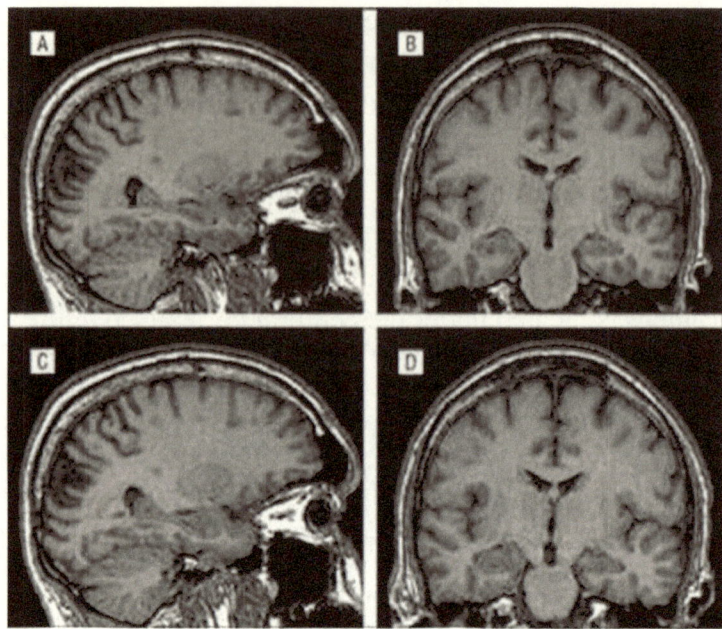

Fig. 50. An MRI showing increased hippocampus size

During his clinical evaluation, it became apparent that he had an unresolved case of survivor's guilt and moral injury. He was experiencing constant painful guilt feelings about surviving the Vietnam War when others did not.

The clinical team spent time clarifying what happened to him, following his acute trauma event when he found that he killed the innocent bicycle riders and the revenge killing that occurred at the orphanage in Saigon. His personal multiple life traumas were overwhelming and prevented trauma reprocessing. As a result, his amygdala with long-term potentiation formed deeply engraved trauma memories. So that severe trauma tape became stuck in his memory.Then, as an attempt to avoid the unbearable pain, numbness occurred to avoid emotionally reexperiencing the trauma and further meaning extraction did not occur, leading to susceptibility for recurrence of these painful intrusive memories.

Survivor's guilt then became a daily self-punishment that he felt he was deserving for the death of the innocents. Since this self-punishment was not sufficient, because he was still able to use his crime instruments, which he has assigned to his left evil eye and left evil hand, then death became a justified and deserved punishment for his unforgivable crimes.

Clinical Neurosciences Study of PTSD

The Clinical Neurosciences Division includes several laboratories specializing in research focused on the physical basis of how the brain receives and processes traumatic stress, including neurobiology, brain imaging, genetic epidemiology, resilience, and pharmacotherapy. The theoretical link between exposure to extreme stress and the development of PTSD provided the rationale for early hypotheses that PTSD-related biological alterations would be similar in direction to those observed acutely in animals exposed to stressors. When subsequent findings indicated that only a minority of trauma-exposed individuals develop PTSD, an alternative hypothesis was generated, proposing that PTSD involves a failure of mechanisms involved in recovery and restitution of physiological homeostasis, possibly resulting from individualistic predisposition.

The hippocampus was examined as a region of central importance in PTSD due to its prominent role in both the neuroendocrine stress response and memory alterations, similar to those that have been observed in PTSD. Many studies have demonstrated smaller hippocampal volumes in PTSD. this led investigators to consider that smaller hippocampal volume represented a preexisting marker of vulnerability to PTSD. The evidence for this possibility is the strong association between hippocampal volume and identical twins discordant for Vietnam combat exposure.

Mr. L insisted that because his MRI showed an increased hippocampus size and normal amygdala size, that these findings were a proof that he did not have PTSD.[30] He wanted to forfeit his benefits and wished to surrender his service connection disability income and the back-payment monies he received for PTSD.

The VA disability review board agreed to consider his request if he can prove employability. He opened a shop to repair and restore old motorcycles, and he financially prospered. A wealthy collector brought him to repair one of his motorcycles and invited him to participate in a special fall festival parade. They practiced the parade several times with no glitches or mishaps.

On the day of the parade, during a wonderful New England beautiful fall weather and the peak of the foliage season, Mr. L rode his motorcycle next to the collector, who wanted to honor him by offering him to ride on the right side of the parade, but he declined and rode on the left side. An unexpected strong wind blew from the left and cluttered the road with fallen tree leaves, and the collector skidded. He tried to prevent his downhill fall by speeding ahead of him, which led Mr.L his own motorcycle accident.

Doctoring 3—University of California Davis School of Medicine

Dr. Denise Kellaher—the director of the Acute Mental Health Care Services at the Sacramento VA Medical Center—Mather, California, conducted a pilot project that pertained to the Emergency Medical Services (EMS) patient transport cart and protocols which led to the implementation of innovating Emergency Psychiatry/ Code Blue Response on VA Hospital

---

30   G. Pavlisa, J. Papa, L. Pavic, et al, "Bilateral MR volumetry of the amygdala in chronic PTSD patients," Coll Antropol (2006), 30:565–568.

premises. Dr. Kellaher graciously offered me a position to join the Sacramento VA medical center where I had the opportunity to work with Drs. David Gellerman and Scott Summers.

Dr. David Gellerman—chief medical director for mental health product line at VA Northern California Health Care System in Mather, California, and associate clinical professor of psychiatry— introduced me to Drs. Michael Wilkes and Shannon Suo. they invited me to volunteer as a faculty facilitator for the Doctoring 3 course for third-year medical students attending the University of California Davis School of Medicine in Sacramento, the capital of California. The course consists of biweekly longitudinal small groups led by faculty members who remain with their group throughout the year as the students rotate through their clerkships. Doctoring 3's themes include advanced interviewing techniques, clinical reasoning, clinical epidemiology, evidence-based medicine, ethics, and jurisprudence. Students use their four-week elective block for clinical clerkships in fields that are not included in the required clerkships but are highly relevant to any discipline such as radiology and neurology. Doctoring 3 is a unique experience that prepares medical students to become the future generation of physicians who need to assimilate the nuances of fast-paced, technically geared, and electronic medical records driven by current medical practice while adhering to the time-honored physician-patient therapeutic and professional relationships. Drs. Joseph Giorgio, Adam Quest, and Anca Luminare were colleagues that also volunteered as Doctoring 3 faculty-facilitators. My involvement in that valuable experience provided me with the opportunity to refresh my rusty knowledge in understanding radiological findings. This allowed me to offer some interpretation to Mr. L in the context of his brain imaging studies. He reflected a listening demeanor but remained silent!

The Posttraumatic Stress Disorder Treatment Program

The Sacramento VA Medical Center in Mather, California, with its Mental Health Services, provides a full range of psychiatric and psychological assessments and interventions, including individual and group psychotherapy, medication management, substance abuse treatment, and posttraumatic stress disorder (PCT) treatment. The PCT program provides specialized treatment for veterans with PTSD. I am grateful that when I Joined the PCT program under the leadership of Dr. **Tanya** Aaen, I had the opportunity to collaborate with a team of devoted clinicians, Drs. Sarah Jackson, Jeannette Giorgio, James Soeffing, Mr. David Ferguson, Ms. Victoria "Vicki" Steen, Mr. Arnold Williams, Mr. Elliot Moore, and Mr. Octavio Rodriguez. The PCT program provides a patient-centered care approach that is individualized based on each veteran's capabilities, needs, goals, prior treatment experiences, and preferences. Veterans are offered access to evidence-based interventions appropriate to their particular and unique presentation of symptoms. This approach challenges the clinicians to educate and clarify available options including the benefits of accepting various treatment modalities and explore any identified treatment barriers. Additionally, the clinicians involve veterans in prioritizing their treatment goals and in setting specific objectives and interventions to achieve these goals. The centered care approach was crucial in guiding my steps in establishing a therapeutic alliance with Mr. L.

Motorcycle Accident and the Parade Aftermath

Mr. L blamed himself for spoiling the parade and wished that he could have died right there and hated his cursed left evil eye, despite the fact that the collector survived that accident, with the exception of few minor arm bruises, while Mr. L suffered a left-eye laceration. Deep inside his soul, he experienced a sense of relief, wishing that, maybe finally, he would lose his left eye and was hoping for a delay in the arrival of the ambulance.

The ultimate goal of Emergency Medical Services (EMS) in New Hampshire is to improve patient safety and high quality out-of- hospital emergency care for everyone. EMS ambulance service provides ground transports for hospitals, urgent care centers, convalescent homes, physicians, insurance companies, fire departments, private and public events. An ambulance was already present at the parade, and its staff provided immediate assistance to Mr. L, and within a span of ten minutes, transported him to the VA hospital emergency department, which subsequently led to his admission to the hospital and to the eye surgery. He wished he could have lost his left eye or even die because that would have been a deserved punishing event coinciding with his forty-fourth birthday.

C H A P T E R 1 6

WHO IS MR. L?

Seven Hours Psychiatry Assessment

Seven hours passed, and I have not seen Mr. L's face. He felt tired, and he wanted to resume sleep. Abruptly and suddenly, his tone of voice changed to a loud shout, announcing that he did not need a shrink and he did not need any long-drawn psychiatric nonsense evaluation and nonscientific interpretation of his dreams and whatever this so-called PTSD was because he did not have it.

He asked me to leave and to not recommend any mental health treatment—the nurses still demanding ongoing psychiatric care and follow- up appointments. I asked about the *Crime and Punishment* book that was next to his bed (see figure 10). He clarified that it was among many books with all his completed assignments that Soeur Marie had left him in the wooden box. He did not know why he experienced an urge to open the box, and he did not recall taking the *Crime and Punishment* book or placing it in his leather motorcycle jacket. He remembered that when he first read it, he experienced the feeling of guilt. He then escalated his voice and repeatedly shouted that he did not need any psychiatric or mental treatment.

I called my chief of service, Dr. Emery (see figure 9), who suggested that I ask Mr. L to tell me more about all the wooden box's books and assignments. He agreed to see me once a month to discuss a book and an assignment. The nurses were not pleased with a monthly follow-up of just discussing books. They contacted the attending surgeon, who agreed with that plan as long as it is a legitimate psychiatric treatment, and asked me what was this obscure treatment.

I answered, "It is bibliotherapy."[31]

I also made a personal commitment to read the same books that Mr. L will discuss during our monthly sessions.

First Bibliotherapy Reading Assignment

Mr. L chose St. Augustine's Life and Legacy. Augustine lived from AD 354 to AD 430, and many of the context of his thoughts were related to the rise and fall of the Roman Empire. His life was profoundly impacted by the death of his concubine and young son. He wrote the City of God to discredit the Roman intellectuals' accusations of Christianity as the cause of Rome's fall and synthesized Christian doctrine with classical philosophy.[32]He described evil as residing in the human will and that no human efforts can undo the consequences of this reality, and as a result, human depravity is in desperate need for atonement.[33]

One can atone through penal substitution to avoid God's wrath by performing daily penance and self-inflicted punishment. Since penal substitution may never be enough, this leads to a life

31   Thomas Editor SP, *Bibliotherapy: New Evidence of Effectiveness, Issues Mental Health Nurse* (2011), 32(4): 191. AND Duncan MK, *J Pediatr Nurs, Creating Bibliotherapeutic Libraries for Pediatric Patients and Their Families: Potential Contributions of a Cognitive Theory of Traumatic Stress* (2010), 25(1): 25–27.

32   Cozby D, *Notes on Bioethics and Sin by Jean-Francois Collange, Christ Bioeth* (2005), 11(2): 183–188.

33   Ibid. and Syed Hassan S. T., Jamaludin H., Latiff L. A., Raman R.A., Khaw W.F., *Mental Trauma Affliction and Infliction: Punishment and Atonement for Sins? Bulletin of Emergency and Trauma* (2014), 2(4): 139–140.

of despair and, ultimately, to an escape and abandonment of the need for atonement. Accordingly, two cities have been formed by two loves—the City of God is defined by its love of God or amor Dei. The City of Man is defined by the love of self or amor sui.[34]

Rome is a case study of the City of Man infected with pride and love for glory. The Romans held it to be shameful for their native land to be in servitude and glorious for it to rule and command. So they devoted their passion and all their energy to maintain their independence and to win world dominion.

The City of God, in contrast, is a community of engagement, transformation, and hope. Following the discussion of this first reading assignment, Mr. L reached the conclusion that America's war in Vietnam was like the many wars fought by Rome and it was a clear example of another City of Man.

According to St. Augustine, two cities are founded on two different loves. The City of Man is consumed by the earthly love of self and will be destroyed by its own deeds and have no hope for atonement. the City of God is focused on the love of God, even to the contempt of self, and is an unattainable utopia. He then said he wanted to die as a punishment for his misdeeds. He just realized that the real punishment would be to prolong his life in order to experience pain and suffering through daily torment. He totally rejected the notion that reconciliation could be granted with God's grace without the need for constant punishment as an essential requirement for atonement.

---

34   Augustine of Hippo, *The City of God, The Two Cities, City of God, Book XIV, Chapter xxviii* (Circa AD 420).

Tulane University—School of Public Health and Tropical Medicine

The Egypt-Israel peace treaty was signed in Washington DC on March 26, 1979, by Egyptian president Anwar Sadat and Israeli Prime Minister Menachem Begin and witnessed by United States President Jimmy Carter. As part of the peace agreement, the US initiated and implemented economic, military, and educational aid to Egypt. The educational aid included peace fellowships offered to recent Egyptian university graduates. Rather than being based on financial need, peace fellowships were merit-based, where graduate students needed to demonstrate a potential for achieving measurable improvements in their projective professional goals. My mother, Jeannette, strongly encouraged me with boundless and confident support to apply for a scholarship to study in the US. I succumbed to her supplication and applied for a scholarship and was selected as a Fulbright scholar of the Hubert H. Humphrey International Fellowship Program. The Tulane University School of Public Health and Tropical Medicine (SPHTM) chose me among other scholars to complete a master's degree in public health (MPH). Following her completion of the residency training in pediatrics at the University of Oklahoma, College of Medicine, Lynn went to SPHTM to obtain the MPH in Maternal and Child Health. I was blessed beyond measures to be found by Lynn in one of the epidemiology classes. I owed all of my married life's joys and endeavors to Lynn. At SPHTM, I was introduced to Dr. Barnett L. Cline, the professor and chair of the Department of Tropical Medicine, who was leading an active teaching and research program with extensive interest on the epidemiology and control of a range of neglected infectious tropical diseases, including schistosomiasis. This infection is known by an eponymous term bilharzia or bilharziasis, as a tribute to Theodor Maximilian Bilharz. He was a German physician who made pioneering discoveries in the field of parasitology. His contributions led to the foundation of tropical medicine. He is best remembered as the discoverer of the blood fluke schistosoma known since ancient times in Egypt. It is a highly prevalent parasitic infection that is transmitted in the water that flows through the Nile River. Bilharzia has devastating effects on the livelihood of many of Egypt's peasants and farmers who solely depend on the Nile River for the irrigation and growing of their year-round crops. For many decades, modern Egypt implemented schistosomiasis control and elimination initiatives which has resulted in reduced prevalence of the disease. Dr. Barnett L. Cline was among the leading researchers in schistosomiasis and had a gracious fondness of Egypt and its medical school graduates studying at SPHTM. He keenly realized and recognized my interests in pursuing a professional career in psychiatry. He introduced me to the Tulane's University Medical School Psychiatry faculty members. These kind and devoted academic psychiatrists encouraged me to pursue a fellowship in cross-cultural psychiatry and anthropology. In an anthropology seminar, the concept of the seven deadly sins and its multidimensional cultural aspects was introduced and elaborated.

The Seven Deadly Sins—a Reprise

The seven deadly sins, also known as the capital vices or cardinal sins, are not literarily mentioned in the Bible and include pride, greed, wrath, envy, lust, gluttony, and sloth.[35] The concept of teaching about the perils of these sins originated with the Desert Fathers and later became fundamental to Catholic Church confessional practices, penitential manuals, sermons, and artworks such as Dante's purgatory where the penitents of Mount Purgatory are grouped and penanced according to their worst sin. The

---

35   Shawn Tucker, *The Virtues and Vices in the Arts: A Sourcebook* (Cascade: 2015), ISBN 978- 1625647184.

Catholic Church used the concept of the deadly sins to curb their evil inclinations before they could fester and corrupt the soul. The seven deadly sins that cry to heaven for vengeance are taught especially in Western Christian traditions as things to be deplored. Mr. L's initial thoughts of revenge against those who tricked him into killing the innocent bicycle riders and the subsequent tragedy that occurred in the orphanage in Vietnam created a constant turmoil in his conscience. Vengeance contradicted all his cherished and endeared memories of Soeur Marie. He unexpectedly recalled that one of his most challenging reading assignments was related to the seven deadly sins. Unbeknown to my conscious awareness, Dr. Cline's gracious welcome to **SPHTM** paved my way to be introduced to the concept of the seven deadly sins. As a result, I could confidently convey to Mr. L that he did not commit the sin of vengeance since, in reality, his plan of revenge was never executed. I could hear a sliver and a glimpse of relief reflected in a whispering statement: "May be so!"

CHAPTER17

ONGOING BIBLIOTHERAPY READING ASSIGNMENTS

Eight years of monthly sessions with all his reading assignments confirmed his firm belief that he deserved no forgiveness. Examples of books that were discussed are summarized in table 4. Mr.L consistently rejected the notion that overcoming the obstacles to his reconciliation with God is possible and that it would not be achieved during his lifetime. Hepatitis C infection continued to be well controlled. He always felt Soeur Marie's presence, especially when he was in a dire need for guidance for his wandering soul.

Table 4. Some of the books that were read during eight years of bibliotherapy sessions

Author	Biography	Publications
Dante Alighier	1308 – 1321	The Divine Comedy
William Shakespeare	1564 – 1616	Hamlet, King Lear, and Macbeth
Victor Hugo	1802 –1885	Les Misérables: Jean Valjean and his experience of redemption
Hans Christian Andersen	1805 – 1875	The Little Mermaid
Charles Dickens	1812– 1870	Oliver Twist
Emily Brontë	1818 – 1848	Wuthering Heights

Jules Verne	1828 – 1905	Around the World in Eighty Days
Leo Tolstoy	1828– 1910	War and Peace
George Bernard Shaw	1856 – 1950	Caesar and Cleopatra, Man and Superman
H.G. Wells	1866 – 1946	The Time Machine
Hermann Hesse	1877 –1962	Siddhartha
Aldous Huxley	1894 – 1963	Brave New World
Ernest Hemingway	(1899 – 1961	The Old Man and the Sea
Gomikawa Junpei	1916– 1995	The Human Condition : No Greater Love Road to Eternity A Soldier's Prayer

I informed him that I will be relocating from New Hampshire to California in three months. Mr.L closed his eyes for a few seconds and just opened his left eye and with his left hand wrote, "It is our final session," and he did not want any more follow-up and assured me he was not intending on dying any time soon because he can only be punished if he was still alive and experiencing daily torment for killing the innocents with his left evil hand using his left evil eye.

Nine Years Hiatus and a Surprise Phone Call

One of my colleagues at the Fresno VA Hospital had to be deployed unexpectedly to Iraq, and he asked me to cover for his weekend of psychiatry on-call duties.

I was paged to answer an out-of-state long-distance phone call. On the other line, a person was greeting me in French, and he challenged me to recognize him. It was Mr. L. He sounded joyful, and he said, "I finally found you."

He asked if I had a few moments to hear his latest news. He then mentioned that he just read a recent article that I published about survivor's guilt and PTSD.[36]By applying the principle of yielding his perceived rights and unmet expectations (see figure 51) rather than feeling resentful and angry, he accepted forgiveness and was amazed that his survivor's guilt did remit, and he eventually understood atonement as described by St. Augustine.[37]He then mentioned that he was currently volunteering at the Ohio VA hospital and that he would send me a detailed email message to update me on his life journey.

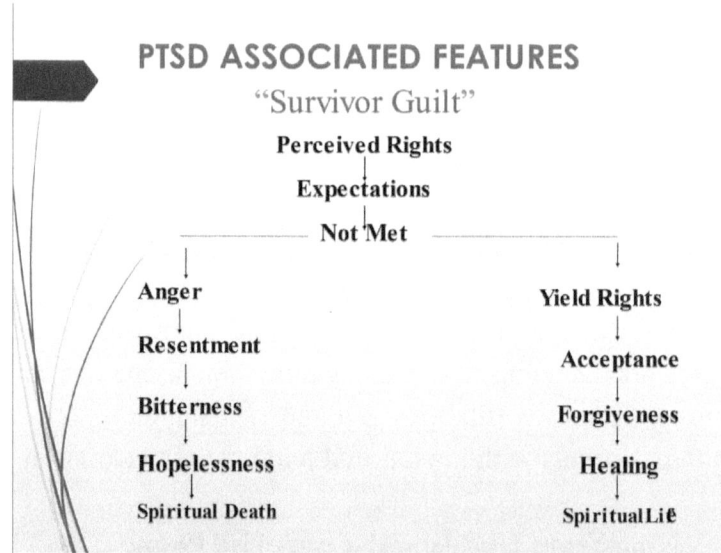

PTSD ASSOCIATED FEATURES
"Survivor Guilt"

Perceived Rights

Expectations

—————— **Not Met** ——————

Anger	**Yield Rights**
Resentment	**Acceptance**
Bitterness	**Forgiveness**
Hopelessness	**Healing**
Spiritual Death	**Spiritual Life**

Fig. 51. Clarification of survivor's guilt

---

36   Khouzam H.R., *Posttraumatic Stress Disorder and Aging, Postgrad Med* (2008), 120(3): 122–129.

37   Ozby D, *Notes on Bioethics and Sin by Jean-Francois Collange, Christ Bioeth* (2005), 11(2): 183–188. and Syed Hassan S.T., Jamaludin H., Latiff L.A., Raman R.A., Khaw W.F., *Mental Trauma Affliction and Infliction: Punishment and Atonement for Sins? Bulletin of Emergency and Trauma* (2014), 2(4): 139–140. AND Augustine of Hippo, *The City of God, The Two Cities, City of God, Book XIV, Chapter xxviii* (Circa AD 420).

The Faculty Leadership Program

The University of Oklahoma Health Sciences Center (OUHSC) Faculty Leadership Program (FLP) is a longitudinal series of highly interactive, small group seminars led by faculty and administrators designed to provide teaching faculty members with an insider's view of their current and future academic missions. Given the scope, complexity, and demanding roles of faculty at a contemporary academic health center, the FLP afforded faculty a structured approach to acquire and apply new skills and to refine existing ones. Grounded in the academic and business literature, the FLP's eleven-month program exposed its participants to both practical and career-focused information, instructional design methods, student assessment techniques, dimensions of university services, and strategies for developing an individualized educational, clinical/ service, and scholarly portfolio. A focus on refining core skills in communication, management, and understanding the impact of university, health sciences, and health care policy on the academic career was provided through the program's leadership dimensions.

Upon its completion, the participants in the FLP gained knowledge and skills in their abilities for critical self-assessment in teaching, scholarship activities, rendering clinical care services, and in providing/ receiving peer-to-peer feedback. The newly appointed chairman of the Department of Psychiatry and Behavioral Sciences at OHHSC, Dr. Joseph Westermeyer, informed the department's junior clinical faculty members that if they wish to teach, supervise, and mentor medical students and psychiatry residents, they would have to be engaged in scholarly activities. Perceiving my love and interests in teaching, Dr. Westermeyer nominated and submitted my name to participate in the FLP. Along with other junior faculty members from medical

173

and surgical disciplines, I graduated from the first and inaugural FLP class by completing over the span of eleven months, a total of 128 continuing professional development hours and a scholarly project. Despite my initial reluctance to accept Dr. Westermeyer's request to join the FLP, his persuasion and support played a pivotal role in the pursuit of scholarly activities, such as publishing in the psychiatric and medical literature. Mr. L tracked and found me after a nine- year hiatus when he read the published article which was initially originated during the FLP at the OHHSC.

A Balint group—a Deeper Appreciation

Balint groups were named after the psychoanalyst Michael Balint (1896–1970).[38]In the late 1950s, Michael and his wife Enid began holding psychological training seminars for general partitioners in London. This work was first described in the book *The Doctor, his Patient, and the Illness* in 1957. Balint encouraged the group members to hold "long interviews" with their most challenging or so-called difficult patients. The groups met once a week for a number of years so that patients and their progress could be followed up. The continuity also enabled group members to feel at ease with each other. Since those early days, Balint groups have spread across the world, and in twenty- two countries, there are national Balint societies, whose aim is to foster.and develop the Balint approach. Dr. Danielle Alexander, a psychiatrist and a faculty member of the Department of Psychiatry and Behavioral Medicine at UC Davis Medical School in Sacramento, California, invited me to join a Balint group that she led. The group was a safe place where to reflect on and to describe the intricate interpersonal aspects of interacting with patients. The members who attended the Balint group sessions were sympathetic and illustrated similar clinical

---

38   Michael Balint. The doctor, his patient, and the illness. Lancet. 1955 Apr 2;268(6866):683-8.

situations they encountered with the patients that they themselves are treating. The various group sessions also encouraged the participants to maintain a constant awareness of the humanity of their patients who have a life and relationships beyond the therapeutic setting. Gradually, the group participants become invested in empathic listening and collectively reached a deeper level of understanding of their patients' feelings and their own. They then realize that certain patients or emotions may resonate with their own inner feelings and their outward manifestations. This then paves the way for the group participants to turn their clinical challenges into therapeutic advantages.

The attendance of the Balint group enabled my appreciation and understanding of Mr. L's personal interpretations of his past and current life stressors.

CHAPTER 18
GRACE AND FORGIVENESS

Mr. L met Grace at the Ohio VA Hospital. She was a Vietnam War nurse. Despite losing both her legs, she was full of love, joy, and hope. He joined her as a volunteer in the department of prosthetics, based on his prosthetic shop experience in Laos. With Grace's experience in applying for grants, they were the recipients of a VA-funded research for designing and creating state-of-the-art prosthetic limbs.

US Nurses during the Vietnam War

The large majority of nurses who served in the Vietnam War were women. Several of the ones who did not die returned home with forever changed lives. The use of helicopters allowed wounded soldiers to reach hospitals much faster than in previous wars. Medevac choppers often picked up, unloaded, and took off again without ever stopping the rotating blades. Such speedy medical evacuation significantly improved the odds of surviving even severe wounds. During the Vietnam War, the number of wounded in combat outnumbered those killed in action by more than six to one. Nurses attending to the injured soldiers witnessed firsthand the horrific seen physical injuries and the unseen emotional wounds of war. The widespread use of assault rifles and rocket-propelled grenades caused severe bodily injuries, and many wounded soldiers lost their limbs, and some became paralyzed. Improvised weapons and booby traps created unique hazards to soldiers and nurses alike. Grace was a victim of crafty set booby trap and eventually had a bilateral below knees amputation. Her faith and commitment uplifted her spirit and guided her to gain a new meaning in life by dedicating her efforts and energy to volunteer. During one of her volunteering assignments, she met Mr.L. He was surprised to witness her limping, and as they conversed, he realized that her prosthesis was not optimally fitted. After several casual meetings, Mr. L offered his expertise and worked diligently on adjusting Grace's prosthesis, and she was able to walk without any limping.

Department of Veterans Affairs (VA) Prosthetic Services

The Department of Veterans Affairs (VA) Prosthetic and Sensory Aids Service (PSAS) is the largest and most comprehensive provider of prosthetic devices and sensory aids in the world. Prosthetics includes artificial limbs and any devices that support or replace a body part or function. VA provides all clinically appropriate and commercially available, state-of-the-art prosthetic equipment, sensory aids, and devices to veterans that cross the full range of patient care. Such items include artificial limbs and bracing; wheeled mobility and seating systems; sensory-neural aids, such as hearing aids and eyeglasses; cognitive prosthetic devices; items specific to women's health; surgical implants, knees, and hips replacement; pacemaker placement; home respiratory care; in addition to recreational and sport equipment. Grace's services during the Vietnam War qualified her to receive services from the PSAS. Mr. L then went on describing his newly gained insight about the concept of grace and forgiveness as conveyed by Grace's own spiritual awakening following the loss of her limbs in Vietnam. He did not need to atone for what he did, witnessed, or experienced during the Vietnam War because reconciliation has occurred through God's grace and forgiveness.

He has proposed to Grace, and she accepted, and then Mr. L paused for few seconds and mentioned that he would be honored if I could attend their wedding. Due to an engagement to providing psychiatric services in a community mental health center in New Zealand, I could not attend the wedding, and he unequivocally accepted my plea! He asked if he could contact me following my return from New Zealand, and I provided him with a date and time. In the meantime, Mr. L, sent a detailed message in which he described a bibliotherapy group that he had initiated under the supervision of a therapist for Vietnam War veterans, who were still suffering from survivor's guilt. The list of books that the group members read monthly over a period of eleven months are summarized in table 5. A year later and on the exact date and time, I received a call from Mr. L, and he asked if I am at liberty to share my work experiences in New Zealand, and so I did.

Table 5. Books used in bibliotherapy sessions for Vietnam War veterans with survivor's guilt*

Author	Book Title	Year of Publication
Shechtman	Aggressiveness	2000
Patricia Irwin Johnston	Adoption/ foster care	2001
Ian McEwan	Atonement *	2007
Muriel James & Dorothy Jongeward	Born to Win*	1973
Elisabeth Kubler-Ross	Death and Dying	1997
Harold E. Doweiko	Chemical dependency	2008
Fritzler, Hecker, & Losee	Obsessive-compulsive disorder	1997
Hebert	Giftedness	1995
Hodges	Conflict resolution	1995

Hannah Green	I Never Promised You a Rose Garden*	1964
Barclay & Whittington	Nightmares	1992
Holman	Ethnic identity	1996
Ackerson, Scogin, Mc Kendree-Smith, Lyman	Depression	1998
Bernstein & Rudman	Separation and Loss	1989
Butterworth & Fulmer	Family violence	1991
Karl Menninger	Man Against Himself*	1956
Farkas & Yorker	Homelessness	1993
Augustine of Hippo, translated by: Albert Cook Outler	St. Augustine Confessions*	2002
by :Thomas Aquinas , Editor: Peter Kreeft	Saint Thomas Aquinas*	1993
M. Scott Peck	The Road Less travelled*	1978
Selma H. Fraiberg	The Magic Years: Understanding and Handling the Problems of Early Childhood*	1977
Tim Hansel	When I Relax I Feel Guilty	1989
Harold S. Kushner	When Bad Things Happen to Good People*	1983

*Books that had the most impact on alleviation of survivor's guilt

Publications addressing PTSD associated features of Survivor's Guilt

1. Gokce G.,Sobaci G.,Ozgonul C.(2015)Post-traumatic endophthalmitis: a mini review. Seminars in Ophthalmology.;30(5-6):470–474.
2. Rabinovich (2004). The Yom Kippur War. Schocken Books. p. 498.
3. New International Version (2012) The Holy Bible. Zondervan, Grand Rapids,MI. (a):Leviticus 23:27,(b): Genesis 15:18.
4. Vatikiotis, PJ. (1992). The History of Modern Egypt (4th edition.). Baltimore: Johns Hopkins University. p. 443
5. Ferini-Strambi L, Zucconi M (2000). REM sleep behavior disorder. Clinical Neurophysiology. 111 Suppl 2: S136–S134
6. Petrushkin HJ, Elgohary MA, Sullivan PM (2015). Rescue pneumatic retinopexy in patients with failed primary retinal detachment surgery. Retina. 35 (9):1851-1859.
7. Charles E. Hummel (1967). tyranny of the Urgent.InterVarsity Christian Fellowship of the USA.Downers Grove, IL.
8. Pereles L, Jackson R, Rosenal T, Nixon L. (2017).Listening with a narrative ear: Insights from a study of fall stories in older adults. Canadian Family Physician. 63(1):E44-E50.
9. Luborsky L(2000). A pattern-setting therapeutic alliance study revisited. Psychotherapy Research . 10:17–29.
10. El-Gabalawi F, Khouzam.HR (2009). The Effect of Mental Illness on Language Regression to the Mother tongue in Bilingual teenagers. J Neuropsychiatry Clin Neurosci 21(1):88-91, 2009.
11. American Psychiatric Association (2013) Diagnostic and Statistical Manual of Mental Disorders (5th edition) Arlington, VA. p.265-268 and p.271-280

12. Boris, Neil W.; Zeanah, Charles H.; Work Group on Quality Issues (2005). Practice parameter for the assessment and treatment of children and adolescents with reactive attachment disorder of infancy and early childhood. Journal of the American Academy of Child and Adolescent Psychiatry. 44 (11): 1206-1219.

13. Krmpotic MD (1908). Dalmatia. Catholic encyclopedia. Retrieved 2008.

14. Paul Ekman,Wallace V. Friesman (2003)Unmasking the Face: A Guide to Recognizing Emotions From Facial Expressions. Malor Books,Los Altos,CA.

15. Robert Plutchik (2002) Emotions and Life: Perspectives from Psychology, Biology, and Evolution, Washington, DC.

16. The Beatles (2000). Anthology. Chronicle Books, Boston, Massachusetts.

17. Schmidt Kt,Weinshenker D (2014) Adrenaline rush: the role of adrenergic receptors in stimulant-induced behaviors. Mol Pharmacol. 85(4):640-50.

18. Veterans of Foreign Wars (VFW) (2015). Encyclopædia Britannica. Retrieved November 14, 2016.

19. E Zach P, Vales K, Stuchlik A, Cermakova P, Mrzilkova J, Koutela A, Kutova M (2016).Effect of stress on structural brain asymmetry.Neuro Endocrinol Lett.37(4):253-264

20. Yehuda R., McFarlane AC (1995) Conflict between current knowledge about posttraumatic stress disorder and its original conceptual basis.Am. J Psychiatry. 152: 1705–1713.

21. Pitman RK, Gilbertson MW, Gurvits TV, May FS, Lasko NB, Metzger L.J, Shenton ME, Yehuda R., Orr SP, and Harvard/VA PTSD(2006) .Twin Study Investigators. Clarifying the origin of biological abnormalities in PTSD through the study of identical twins discordant for combat exposure. Ann. N Y Acad. Sci. 1071: 242–254.

22. Bremner JD (2007) .Functional neuroimaging in post-traumatic

stress disorder. Expert Rev. Neurother. 7: 393–405.

23. Thomas Editor SP(2011). Bibliotherapy: new evidence of effectiveness. Iissues Ment Health Nurs. 32(4):191.

24. Duncan MK(2010).Creating bibliotherapeutic libraries for pediatric patients and their families: potential contributions of a cognitive theory of traumatic stress. J Pediatr Nurs. 25(1):25-27.

25. Cozby D (2005). Notes on "bioethics and sin" by Jean-Francois Collange. Christ Bioeth. 11(2):183-188.

26. Syed Hassan ST, Jamaludin H, Latiff LA, Raman RA, Khaw WF (2014). Mental trauma Affliction and Infliction: Punishment and Atonement for Sins?Bull Emerg trauma. 2(4):139-140.

27. Augustine of Hippo (Circa 420 A.D).the City of God The two Cities, City of God, Book XIV, Chapter xxviii,

28. Khouzam HR (2008).Posttraumatic stress disorder and aging. Postgrad Med. 120(3): 122-129.

Matariki—Auckland, New Zealand

The Matariki Community Mental Health Center serves the population of Ōtāhuhu, Ōtara, and Māngere regions of South Auckland in New Zealand. One of its main missions is to provide culturally sensitive, accessible, and quality mental health and addiction services for people aged eighteen to sixty-five years of age. Its interdisciplinary treatment team is wide in its cultural background and its staff members, which include nurses, psychiatrists, clinical psychologists, social workers, occupational therapists, peer support specialists, clinical nurse specialists, dual diagnosis clinicians, supported employment consultants, and cultural support staff. The center offers a wide range of psychosocial interventions and evidence-based treatments that are tailored to meet individual and family needs.

Commonly provided services included information and education about mental health issues and treatment options, psychological therapies, pharmacological treatment, and referral to specialized psychiatric services. Individual, group, and family therapies are also provided. For patients whose English is a second language, accommodation for interpreters is readily available. I had the opportunity to work as a consultant psychiatrist at Matariki with the interdisciplinary treatment team that is caring for Mr. A, a young adult Māori gentleman, who was considered a difficult to treat patient based on long history of nonadherence with recommended treatment for repeated episodes of depression and daily use of marijuana. Although he was fluent in English, he always insisted on being accompanied by an interpreter to translate his statements from Māori to English. The Māori language is spoken to some extent by about a fifth of all Māori, representing three percent of their total New Zealand's (Aotearoa) population. The Māori originated with settlers from East Polynesia, who arrived in New Zealand in several waves of canoe voyages between roughly 1320 and 1350. Over several centuries in isolation, these settlers developed their own distinctive culture, whose language, mythology, crafts, and performing arts evolved independently from those of other eastern Polynesian cultures. Māori were forced to assimilate into many aspects of Western culture. Social upheaval and epidemics of introduced disease took a devastating toll on dramatically decreasing their population. Disproportionate numbers of Māori face significant economic and social obstacles and generally have lower life expectancies and incomes compared with other New Zealand ethnic groups. They also suffer higher levels of health problems and educational under- achievement. By the start of the twentieth century, the Māori population begun to recover, and ongoing efforts have been made to increase their standing in the wider New Zealand society. I intently attempted to ignore listening to the English translation of

Mr. A's narratives. I wanted to lend my ears to empathic listening to his plights and his emotions rather than being distracted by words and long English sentences. A stream of tears came down his cheeks, which prompted the interpreter to frantically reach for the nearest box of tissue papers. That outward expression of care was swiftly rejected by Mr. A, who started to speak fluently in English announcing that he hated the orphanage. Total silence engulfed the room. He gently apologized, whipped his tears, and over a two hour span, described in canny and elaborate details the emotional pain that he endured in an orphanage following the disappearance of his parents who never returned from a family trip to the Island of Samoa. He reportedly was constantly pressured to abandon his Māori language and forced to only speak in English. Although these practices are currently prohibited and there are no more orphanages in New Zealand, his vacated orphanage building still existed, and its remnants were recently described on a tourist brochure. Mr. A came for several follow-up appointments and attended individual psychotherapy sessions for treatment of depression and participated in the substance abuse treatment program at the Matariki Community Mental Health Center. Additionally, he chose to attend nonmandatory educational classes that I taught about the biopsychosocial and spiritual dimensions of various psychiatric conditions. Over a three month span, he gradually and eventually stopped using marijuana and experienced marked improvement and remission of depression. I was forevermore enriched by the depth of his human insights and artistic talents in sculpture. Prior to my return to the US, Mr. A gave me a wooden carved Kiwi bird (see figure 52), which is the national New Zealand bird. No adequate words could sufficiently express my sincere gratitude of thankfulness for Mr. A's graciousness in giving me that unique hand-crafted bird and in granting me the permission to share his life's story with Mr. L.

Fig. 52. A hand-crafted kiwi bird

I could hear Mr. L's choking voice. There were a few silent pauses, then joyful sighs, followed by a tender loving expression: "After all being said and done, Mr. A's life's and mine are different yet similar. We have been together all along although we never met!"

C H A P T E R 1 9

BACK TO THE BEGINNING

Mr. L early childhood was overshadowed by his survival instinct and driven by self-preservation and self-centeredness, He was overwhelmed by the nurturing and unconditional love of the Carmelite nun Soeur Marie. Under her persuasive and gentle guidance, he was able to excel in expressing his God's given innate talents. He experienced a rebirth and a transformed life. Selfishness, anger, and aggressive tendencies turned to outward manifestation of faith, hope, and love. Driven by patriotism and duties to serve, he fulfilled his military mission as a sniper during the Vietnam War with outstanding valor and dedication. He extended his compassion to help another nun, Sister Marie Nguyen, in providing food and protection to Vietnamese orphans. He was tricked and subsequently killed the innocents and succumbed to the destructive influences of posttraumatic stress disorder associated feature of survivor guilt and was set about a self-destructive and perilous journey to atone for his evil deeds. Grace found him in the midst of his ultimate desperation, and he underwent a spiritual awakening and rebirth. Brokenness was once again transformed to a new life journey of faith, hope, and bountiful love. All along his journey of heartaches, overwhelming emotional, pain and soul-piercing guilt, Mr. L challenged my personal deep-held religious beliefs, historical heritage, clinical knowledge, academic calling, and my preconceived notions about humanity and the plights of the poor, the disfranchised and the unremitting battles against the "evils" of the world. The initial resentment of pursuing an unwarranted psychiatric consultation opened a gate of wondrous and inspiring reflections to honor past and present family members, friends, teachers, mentors, and colleagues for their indispensable contributions to my personal and professional growth and my voyages with storytelling.

The Road That Connects Karnak to Luxor and Psychiatry in Ancient Egypt

The Karnak temple Complex was the center of the ancient faith of the Egyptians, while the governing of Egypt was concentrated at Thebes, which is modern-day Luxor. These are cherished sites for my sister Hoda, who is an Egyptologist and a scholar of hieroglyphics. She has, on many occasions, clarified the majestic significance of Karnak and Luxor as reflected in their enormous and monumental structures. In addition to their religious importance, these monumental structures served as treasury, administrative center, and palace for the New Kingdom pharaohs. It is, to this day, considered the largest temple complex ever constructed anywhere in the world (see figure 53). They developed over a period of 1,500 years, added by generation after generation of pharaohs and resulting in a collection of temples, sanctuaries, pylons, and other decorations that are unparalleled throughout Egypt.

Fig. 53. The road that connects Karnak to Luxor during a
"sound and sight" night presentation

While the height of their importance was during the New
Kingdom and the reigns of famous pharaohs, such as Hatshepsut,
Tuthmose III, Seti I, and Ramesses II, other pharaohs contributed
significant additions to the complex and continued construction of
the Greco-Roman Period with the Ptolemies, Romans, and early
Christians, all leaving several of their marks on the temple
walls and columns. During my medical school years, along with
my dear friends Salah, Fouad, Essam, and Alyaa, we spent time
visiting these historical monuments. We reflected back on the many
generations who could have witnessed, lived, or participated in the
magnificent events that occurred within the walls of Karnak and
Luxor. Our hearts and mind were pricked, wondering if psychiatry,
as a medical discipline, was practiced during that period of Egypt's
history. Fortunately, Ancient Egyptians documented all of their
life details on stone carving, clay, or papyri.

Papyri, the plural word for papyrus, is a material similar to thick
paper that was used in ancient times as a writing surface and made

from the pith of the papyrus plant. Papyri also refer to documents written on sheets of such material, joined side by side and rolled up into a scroll, which is an early form of a book. Although many of Ancient Egypt's records have been lost or destroyed, the surviving documents represent invaluable sources of knowledge in the different scientific aspects of medical practice in Ancient Egypt. Most relevant to psychiatry is Edwin Smith's papyri, which he bought in 1862 and is set to describe events around 1550 BC. In the papyri, the brain is described for the first time in history as being enclosed in a membrane, and its hemispheres are patterned with convolutions.

The Ancient Egyptians recognized that the brain was the site of mental functions. They emphasized the importance of assessing the state of consciousness and memory in all routine medical examinations. The state of consciousness was commonly expressed in phrases such as "the perishing of the mind," "the mind is forgetful like one who is thinking of something else," "the fleeting mind," "the mind goes away," and "it is difficult to hear the spoken word." These descriptions seem to be rather comparable to the way patients are able to concentrate and maintain their attention. The Egyptians also believed that every personality had a part, which was the "sum" of the real or inner self. This explains their belief in the principle of the two names: one is known, and the other is hidden. The real name of the person was identified with the person himself. *"Nothing existed that had not received a name and who lost his name, lost his personality, and independence."*[39]

This bears a keen resemblance to the Freudian concept of the "unconscious" or the concept of the invisible in Gestalt psychology. The struggle to know the real name was symbolic

---

39   Maspero [1912] *Guide du Visileur au Musee del Caire.* Printed by Inst. Fr. d' Arch Or, Cairo, Und ed. 6, 507.

of the struggle to know the unknown. Another papyrus narrates, "I am he who has names. My mother and my father told me my name. It is hidden since my birth in my body." Mr. L pondered in several of our bibliotherapy sessions if he had a birth name that was changed when he was placed in the orphanage. He would imagine various life scenarios associated with different birth names, then ascertain that most probably, no matter what birth name he had, his destiny would have remained unchanged. He would respond to my silent pauses by reminding me that his deep-rooted belief in Soeur Marie's unconditional love would always anchor his mind back to the safety of another memorized verse: *"Before I formed you in the womb, I knew you, and before you were born, I consecrated you"* (Jeremiah 1:5).

The Eye of Horus

Thinking about my city of birth, Heliopolis, which was the original name of the capital of Ancient Lower Egypt, reminded me of its association with the eye of Horus. Horus is one of the most Ancient Egyptian deities and is one of the most important gods in the Egyptian pantheon. He is most often depicted with a falcon's head and is crowned with the pschent, the emblem of the pharaohs of Egypt (see figure 54). Horus became the protective deity of the pharaohs and kings of Egypt because they were the guarantor of universal harmony on earth, while Horus was the guarantor of universal harmony in the afterlife. Horus was also considered the god of the sky and celestial spaces. Horus was worshipped in both Upper and Lower Egypt.

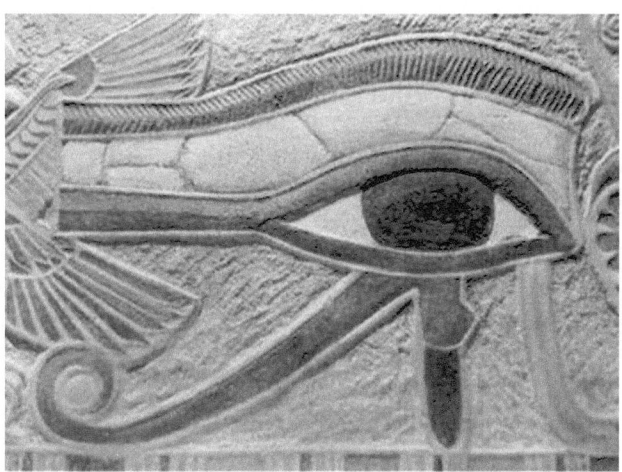

Fig. 54. A replica of the Eye of Horus

The oldest city to have Horus as its protector is Nekhen, translated literally as "City of the Falcon." Horus was also highly venerated in Heliopolis, "City of the Sun," the ancient capital of Lower Egypt. The circumstances of Horus's birth are narrated in the myth of Osiris, which stems from the fraternal jealousy of Set toward Osiris. On the other hand, we find Osiris considered by all as the perfect being, and on the other hand, we find Set, a representation of evil and disarray. This jealousy was fueled by two events:

First, the appointment of Osiris as a worthy heir of Ra to the throne of Egypt.

Secondly, Set's wife, Nephthys, bewitched by the charm and presence of Osiris, pretended to be Isis, his wife, in order to have a child with him. From this forbidden union, Anubis was born. Set's resentment toward his brother will lead to his murder. The murder of Osiris is one of the most popular myths of Ancient Egypt, both in its realization and its outcome. During a banquet, Set decides to trap his brother. He offered all the guests the chance to take part in a game, with a priceless chest winnable at the end of the game.

191

The rules were simple: whoever manages to get into the priceless chest wins. Previously cut to Osiris's dimensions, he was naturally the only one who was able to get into it. However, as soon as Osiris was inside, Set closed the lid of the chest and threw it into the Nile, causing his brother to drown. This chest then became the first sarcophagus in Egypt. Isis immediately set off in search of her husband's body. Once the body was found, using her healing powers, she tried to bring him back to life, which proved to be futile. Instead, their son, the falcon-headed god Horus, was born from the strength of Isis's love for Osiris.

Set then decided to cut the body of his brother into fourteen separate pieces and scattered them throughout Egypt. With no more pretenders to the throne, Set seized power and became king of Egypt. Isis then led an expedition in order to find each fragment of Osiris's body and succeeded in gathering and assembling Osiris's body. Combining her powers with those of her sister, she brought Osiris back to life, who then became the god of the kingdom of the dead. Horus sought to avenge his father and recover the power usurped by his uncle, Set. After many years of terror on the throne of Egypt, Horus summoned a divine jury composed of Ra (the god of the solar disc), Thoth (the god of wisdom), and Shu (the god of air) to decide on the lawful king. The three deities decided that Set (as the brother of Osiris) and Horus (as the son of Osiris) were both entitled to the throne and that the two rivals must face each other in trials in order to show their ability to rule Egypt. However, Set showed disloyalty at every confrontation and used cunning and deception to win all the completed trials.

Before the last trial, Horus decided to rest on the top of a mountain. Set took advantage of Horus's sleep to tear out his left eye and split it into six pieces, which he threw into the Nile. Thoth then decided to find each sliver of Horus's eye to reconstitute it. He only found five pieces and chose to replace the last missing fragment with a divine particle. The six pieces combined together then became the Eye of Horus and allowed Horus to see beyond the visible. Equipped with his divine reconstructed left eye, Horus triumphed in the final confrontation. Set was then banished to the desert, his initial kingdom, and began his long journey of repentance. Horus became king of Egypt and married Hathor, the goddess of love and beauty. Mr. L seemed to marvel at the reconstruction of Horus's left eye.

My mind pondered, *could some unexpected events lead to a transformation of his perception of his left eye as being an evil eye that deserved to be destroyed?* Then with a punctuated sigh, he unexpectedly affirmed that his left eye was the one that caught glimpses of Grace and her beauty! Although I was curious and tempted to inquire if reconciliation had occurred and that he has come to terms with cherishing his left eye, I was at a loss of words and chose to move on and live with the assumption that Mr. L has accepted his left eye as a gift of the goodness of God.

Mr. L then asked if he could sing "I Have a Maker," a song composed by Tommy Walker. He mentioned that Grace used to sing it when she felt that he was isolated and withdrawn.

I have a Maker He formed my heart Before even time began My life was in his hands,
He knows my name He knows my every thought He sees each tear that falls And He hears me when I call,
I have a Father He calls me His own He'll never leave me No matter where I go,
He knows my name He knows my every thought He sees each tear that falls And He hears me when I call,
He knows me, He knows my name He knows my name He knows my every thought,

He sees each tear that falls And He hears me when I call.

Mr. L then remarked that he is contemplating purchasing a left-handed guitar, and with Grace, who plays the clarinet, they plan on singing that song while volunteering for charitable organizations that raise funds for orphanages worldwide. With a low and soft distinct voice, he uttered, "Playing the guitar will ultimately transform my left-hand evil nature into a doer of good deeds." I was profoundly impressed by Mr. L's gained appreciation of his left-hand new mission of becoming an instrument of good deeds. This revelation stood in a formidable contrast to his original perception of his left hand as being an evil hand that killed the innocents in Vietnam.

Rural Mental Health Care

During a session Mr. L asked me if I listened to a national podcast about community mental health centers in rural America. I was surprised by his inquiry, and commented that the VA health care system pioneered and set in motion the trend of integrating and distributing more services from centralized medical centers to clinics near the homes where Veterans live and inaugurated over 800 Community-Based Outpatient Clinics (CBOCs) that facilitate and expediate access to quality health care services. These clinics provide outpatient medical services, including mental health and wellness programs to many rural locations such as the Central California Valley. The CBOC network of rural clinics are also equipped to deliver virtual and telehealth care which was essential during and in the aftermath of the global Covid-19 pandemic. Mr. L then, drew parallels and described comparisons between rural New Hampshire and rural Central California and expressed his keen awareness of the importance of rural hospitals as cornerstones of their communities, serving as key access points of care for nearly 20% of the US population. Additionally, he clarified that beyond their direct impact on health and well-being, rural hospitals also offer broader societal benefits, since they are often the largest local employer which help attract other businesses to their locations and thus contribute to the economic stability of the population residing in these communities. He also elaborated that his studies in civic history have demonstrated that during time of economic downturns, many rural health care facilities would face financial challenges and a concerning number of them would have to shut their doors. With each hospital and clinic closure, patients then would lose their access to essential services, and local economies are significantly impacted. Few years later I recalled Mr. L unexpected revelations and knowledge about rural health care, which reminded me to express my gratitude to the Fresno VA Central California Health Care System (VACCHCS) rural mental health clinics team. These clinics are organized and lead by Dr. Kathryn Connolly, with Dr. Bradley Norlander, and team members Drs. Neil Smith, Shwetha Katta, Nader Nassar, Cindy Duncan, Maxim Kramer, Paul Pasion Gonzales, Tara Cummings, and Jann Dodd, Social Worker Ms. Rachel Sprunger, Marital and Family Therapist Mr. Brian Campany, the Registered Nurses, Mr. Mark Sevilla, and Mr. Aleksey Vasilenko, and the Administrative Assistants, Ms. Ashley Jones, Ms. Racquel Maximo, Ms. Nancy Vue and Ms. Maria Cristina Madrigal and their back-up Ms. Jowaunna Hearne, Ms. Blanca Weidenbach, Ms. Tiffany Va, Ms. Irene Zambrano, and Mr. Alfred Stephens. The rural mental health clinics multidisciplinary treatment team strives to deliver efficient and compassionate mental health treatment to the many Veterans who reside in the various counties of rural Central California in the San Joaquin Valley. The team has been recognized as an exemplary model of practicing collaborative and comprehensive mental health treatment in an environment of care that fosters trust, and encourages uniqueness and respect among all of its clinical and administrative staff.

Andrew Lloyd-Webber—The keys to open up the Vaults of Heaven

Mr. L described Soeur Marie and her life's legacy as a universe of unconditional love, marvels and awes. He cherished being called her precious little boy and her affirmation that his light blue eyes would someday open up the keys to the vaults of heaven. He joyfully proclaimed that the bright shining lights of hope, forgiveness and love are the keys that opened his vaults of heaven. With his beloved wife Grace and with Soeur Marie everlasting protection, his soul was liberated from the darkness of shame, and the torments of guilt and despair. I could barely control a flow of tears until I got home and rushed to my CD player and listened to the song "vaults of heaven".

Keys to the vaults of heaven
May be buried somewhere in a prayer
The Keys to the vaults of heaven
May be heavy or lighter than air

Open up the vaults
Open up the vaults
We've got to find the keys

The nights have been growing darker
Even darker now than sin
We'll open the vaults of heaven
The treasures are there within

The keys to the vaults of heaven
May be seen in a pure child's eyes
The keys to the vaults of heaven
May be heard in our desperate cries

Open up the vaults
Open up the vaults
We've got to find the keys

The nights have been growing darker
Even darker now than sin
We'll open the vaults of heaven
The glories are there within

I did not know whether Mr. L was familiar with the origin of the term open up the vaults of heaven from the musical *Whistle Down the Wind*, which was composed and co-written by Andrew Lloyd-Webber, the English composer and impresario of musical theatre. Several of his musicals have run for more than a decade both in the West End of London and on Broadway in New York City. He has composed 21 musicals, a song cycle, a set of variations, two film scores, and a Latin Requiem Mass. He was appointed Knight Bachelor in 1992 for his services to the arts and in 1997 he was created a life peer as Baron Lloyd-Webber, of Sydmonton in the County of Hampshire. He is properly styled as The Lord Lloyd-Webber and sat as a Conservative member of the House of Lords until his retirement in October of 2017. In the course of the opening scene of the musical *Whistle Down the Wind*, there is a depiction of a small church in Louisiana where on Christmas Eve, the congregation sang the "Vaults of Heaven". I was overwhelmed with warmth and serenity visualizing Soeur Marie seeing the keys to the vaults of heaven in Mr. L pure child's eyes and predicting that heaven glories are tucked within his heart.

Lessons Learned—The Commencement

Mr. L's narratives, his life story launched a platform to convey to colleagues, friends, family, and all the patients that cross my path that forgiveness is possible. No matter what happened and despite survivor's guilt, posttraumatic stress disorder (PTSD), hopelessness, and despair; faith, hope, and love could be restored. St. Augustine's personal experience with atonement and other bibliotherapy avenues could be contemplated as road maps for lifelong spiritual journey to achieve forgiveness and everlasting healing, even in the face of indescribable adversity, unbearable emotional pain, and excruciating mental agony.

Traditionally the patient-physician relationship is perceived as being mostly one-sided, with physicians educating, instructing, and recommending treatment to their patients who must accept with minimal input. The unique and powerful relationship between patients and physicians discredits and undermines the fact that physicians can learn from their patients if they perceive them as an open book with unique genetic, socioeconomic, personal narratives, and storytelling characteristics. The importance of this knowledge was captured by physicians of the earlier civilizations of Egypt, Greece, and Rome and eloquently described in the twentieth century notable physician and professor of medicine Dr. William Osler's statement that "he who studies medicine without books sails an uncharted sea, but he who studies medicine without patients does not go to sea at all." Listening to Mr. L sharing his journey of rewards and tragedies allowed me to experience a unique perspective of an amazing life of triumphs over defeats. Mr. L taught me to be always present in the moment and to be willing to accept what life has to offer, and I am grateful for the opportunity he offered to challenge my preconceived notions about the best practices in psychiatric treatment. By participating and discussing the various reading assignments, he broadened my views of the uniqueness of each individual regardless of the nature of their illness. He has caused me to increasingly value the human connections that are essential to maintaining hope, faith, and love.

He brought into focus the fragility of life and our vulnerability to emotional discomfort that we all share, physicians and patients alike, and the anxieties and fears each of us face when confronted by practical and unsurmountable heart breaking circumstances. In the midst of each session, I felt compelled to examine my own response to life's inevitable difficulties. Having the opportunity to travel mentally along with Mr. L as he describes the irreversibility of death has also challenged me to confront my own mortality and think of how I want and hope that process will occur for me and how it will impact my loved ones. And perhaps most importantly, observing his strength and resilience in dealing with adversity has provided me with important lessons about valuing life and attempting to live each day to its fullest. His narratives and stories were a great source of personal enrichment and inexpressible spiritual growth.

Overwhelmed by a deeply felt gratitude and thankfulness, I promised Mr. L to share his life legacy to which he graciously agreed. I have told his story of redemption to various audiences in the states of New Hampshire, Oklahoma, Maine, Missouri, California, Pennsylvania, New York, Vermont, Florida, Virginia, Oregon and Washington, and the countries of Egypt, Canada, England, and New Zealand.

ABOUT THE AUTHOR

For years I dreamed about writing a book of stories that describe the many triumphs of the human spirit over the burdens of adversity, brokenness, and suffering.

As an Egyptian and a Naturalized American Citizen, I was showered with the cultural and scientific blessings of one of the oldest and the youngest human civilizations.

Being a grandson, a son, a brother, a cousin, a nephew, an uncle, a husband, a father, a grandfather, a friend and a colleague brought me countless stories of hope over despair, healing in the midst of pain, unconditional love and forgiveness in response to inflicted and perpetrated wounds.

The clinical experiences as a physician, a psychiatrist, and an academician provided me with awe-inspiring moments of listening to patients' narratives and trainees' challenges as they interlude with their daily journey of learning and healing.

The dream became a reality with this first storytelling book which attempts to portray the power that flows from accepting adversities as boundless opportunities to connect with the essence of humanity and faith in the divine.

For that I remain indefinitely humble and grateful.

www.ingramcontent.com/pod-product-compliance
Lightning Source LLC
Chambersburg PA
CBHW020238130626
46549CB00005B/1954